# R Machine Learning Essentials

Gain quick access to the machine learning concepts and practical applications using the R development environment

**Michele Usuelli**

BIRMINGHAM - MUMBAI

# R Machine Learning Essentials

First published: November 2014

Production reference: 1211114

Published by Packt Publishing Ltd.
Livery Place
35 Livery Street
Birmingham B3 2PB, UK.

ISBN 978-1-78398-774-0

www.packtpub.com

# Credits

**Author**
Michele Usuelli

**Reviewers**
Eric Hare
Jithin S L
Jia Liu
Samir Madhavan
Raghavendra Prasad Narayan
Owen S. Vallis

**Acquisition Editor**
Subho Gupta

**Content Development Editor**
Amey Varangaonkar

**Technical Editor**
Mrunmayee Patil

**Copy Editors**
Alfida Paiva
Rashmi Sawant
Laxmi Subramanian

**Project Coordinator**
Leena Purkait

**Proofreaders**
Simran Bhogal
Ameesha Green
Paul Hindle

**Indexer**
Monica Ajmera Mehta

**Graphics**
Abhinash Sahu

**Production Coordinator**
Alwin Roy

**Cover Work**
Alwin Roy

# About the Author

**Michele Usuelli** is a data scientist living in London. He has a background of and is passionate about statistics and computer science, and as part of his work, he has explored different software and tools for data analysis and machine learning, focusing on R.

Always wanting to share what he learned from his projects, Michele has written some articles on R-bloggers. R connected to Hadoop and some applications of R tools are the topics covered here.

Michele is passionate about cutting-edge technologies and fast-paced growing environments. Since the very beginning, his work took place in start-up environments. He started his career in one of the most innovative big data start-ups in Milan and worked for a top publishing company in the pricing and analytics division. Currently, he works for a leading R-based company.

I wouldn't have been able to write this book without my personal and professional growth in the last few years, and so I would like to thank all the people I worked with, and of course, my family and friends. I have worked with great people and learned a lot from them.

# About the Reviewers

**Eric Hare** is a graduate from the Department of Statistics at Iowa State University. He graduated from the University of Washington in 2012 with a Bachelor's degree in Statistics and in Computer Engineering. He does research in statistical graphics, statistical computing, and data manipulation. He is currently working on a web application to analyze the statistical properties of Peptide Libraries.

**Jithin S L** completed his B.Tech in Information Technology from Loyola Institute of Technology and Science. He started his career in the field of analytics and then moved to various verticals of big data technology. He has worked with reputed organizations such as Thomson Reuters, IBM Corporation, and Flytxt, under different roles. He has worked in the banking, energy, healthcare, and telecom domains, and has handled global projects on big data technology.

He has submitted many research papers on technology and business at national and international conferences.

In Albert Einstein's words, *learn from yesterday, live for today, hope for tomorrow. The important thing is not to stop questioning.*

I surrender myself to God Almighty who helped me throughout these days to review this book in an effective way.

I dedicate my work on this book to my dad, Mr. N. Subbian Asari (late), my lovable mom, Mrs. M. Lekshmi, and my sweet sister, Ms. S.L Jishma, for coordinating and encouraging me to produce this book.

Last but not least, I would like to thank all my friends.

**Jia Liu** obtained her PhD degree in Statistics from Iowa State University. Her research interests are in mixed-effects model, Bayesian method, Bootstrap method, reliability, design of experiments, machine learning, and data mining. She has 3 years of working experience in the pharmaceutical industry.

**Samir Madhavan** has extensive experience in big data and machine learning. He has worked for the ubiquitous Unique Identification Project, Aadhar, where he was part of the team that helped in developing its fraud module. He was also part of the initial team when Flutura Decision Sciences and Analytics started off. He has created various analytical products, which are being used by the e-commerce, retail, and M2M industries.

**Raghavendra Prasad Narayan** has completed his Bachelor of Engineering in Electronics and Communication from VTU, Belgaum, and completed his Master's degree majoring in Knowledge Engineering from the National University of Singapore. Since 2009, his area of work has been machine learning and natural language processing (NLP). He has worked on the different problems of NLP, and to solve these problems, he has used the ML algorithms extensively (such as classification, clustering algorithms, feature selection/reduction methods, and graphical models). Other than NLP problems, he has also worked on social network analysis, stock market forecasting, yield predictions, and market mix modeling problems.

Currently, he is working at Meltwater Group in the Data Enrichment team as an NLP engineer.

**Owen S. Vallis** is currently a professor of Music Technology for the *Music Technology: Interaction, Intelligence, and Design* program at the California Institute of Arts. Owen is a musician, artist, and scientist interested in performance, sound, and technology. As a cofounder of Flipmu and The Noise Index, he explores a diverse range of projects including big data research and sound art installations. He produces, composes, and designs audio processors, and creates new hardware interfaces for musical performance.

Owen received his PhD in 2013 from the New Zealand School of Music, Victoria University, Wellington, and explored contemporary approaches to live computer music. During his graduate research, Owen focused on developing new musical interfaces, interactive musical agents, and large networked music ensembles. Owen graduated as a Bachelor of Arts in Music Technology from the California Institute of the Arts in 2008.

Having lived in Toronto, Canada; Wellington, New Zealand; Tokyo, Japan; San Francisco; Nashville; and Los Angeles; Owen has been able to develop a broad and interesting cross section of musical ideologies and aesthetics. Over the past 10 years, he has worked as a research scientist for Twitter; developed multitouch interfaces for Nokia research labs; worked for the leading ribbon microphone manufacturer Royer Labs; has had musical production featured in major motion films; built a recording facility; and produced, engineered, and mixed records in Tokyo, Nashville, and Los Angeles. Owen's work has been featured in Wired, Future Music, Pitchfork, XLR8R, Processing.org, and various computer arts magazines, and is shown at events such as NASA's Yuri's Night, Google I/O, and the New York Cutlog art festival.

# www.PacktPub.com

## Support files, eBooks, discount offers, and more

For support files and downloads related to your book, please visit www.PacktPub.com.

Did you know that Packt offers eBook versions of every book published, with PDF and ePub files available? You can upgrade to the eBook version at www.PacktPub.com and as a print book customer, you are entitled to a discount on the eBook copy. Get in touch with us at service@packtpub.com for more details.

At www.PacktPub.com, you can also read a collection of free technical articles, sign up for a range of free newsletters and receive exclusive discounts and offers on Packt books and eBooks.

https://www.packtpub.com/books/subscription/packtlib

Do you need instant solutions to your IT questions? PacktLib is Packt's online digital book library. Here, you can search, access, and read Packt's entire library of books.

## Why subscribe?

- Fully searchable across every book published by Packt
- Copy and paste, print, and bookmark content
- On demand and accessible via a web browser

## Free access for Packt account holders

If you have an account with Packt at www.PacktPub.com, you can use this to access PacktLib today and view 9 entirely free books. Simply use your login credentials for immediate access.

# Table of Contents

# Preface

When facing a business problem, machine learning allows you to develop powerful and effective data-driven solutions. The recent explosion of data volume and sources increased the effectiveness of solutions based on data, so this field is becoming more and more valuable. Developing a machine learning solution has specific requirements, and there are some software and tools that support it. A very good option is to use R, which is an open source programming language for statistics supported by a wide international community. The R structure is projected for statistical analysis, and the international community develops the most cutting-edge solutions. For these reasons, R allows you to develop powerful machine learning solutions using just a few lines of code.

There are machine learning tutorials, and they usually require some knowledge of the basics of statistics and computer science. This book is not just a tutorial. It doesn't even require a strong background in statistics or computer science. The target is not to provide you with a complete overview of all the techniques or to teach you how to build sophisticated solutions. This book is a path full of hands-on examples that provide you with the expertise to build a solution to a new problem. The aim is to show the most important concepts behind the approach in such a way that you have a deep understanding of machine learning and are able to identify and use the new algorithms.

## What this book covers

*Chapter 1, Transforming Data into Actions*, shows you how new technologies allow you to solve business problems with a data-driven approach.

*Chapter 2, R – A Powerful Tool for Developing Machine Learning Algorithms*, explains why R is a great option for machine learning, and covers the basics of the software.

*Chapter 3, A Simple Machine Learning Analysis*, shows you a simple example of machine learning solutions.

*Chapter 4, Step 1 – Data Exploration and Feature Engineering*, shows you how to clean and transform the data before using machine learning algorithms.

*Chapter 5, Step 2 – Applying Machine Learning Techniques*, shows you how to apply machine learning algorithms to solve the problem.

*Chapter 6, Step 3 – Validating the Results*, shows you how to measure an algorithm's accuracy in order to tune its parameters.

*Chapter 7, Overview of Machine Learning Techniques*, presents the main branches of machine learning algorithms.

*Chapter 8, Machine Learning Examples Applicable to Businesses*, shows you how to solve a business problem using machine learning.

# What you need for this book

The only software that you need to run the code is R, preferably 3.0.0+. It is highly recommended, although not necessary, that you install the RStudio Desktop IDE.

# Who this book is for

This book is intended for those who want to learn how to perform some machine learning using R, in order to gain insight from their data and to find the solution to some real-life problems. Perhaps you already know a bit about machine learning but have never used R, or perhaps you know a little R but are new to machine learning. In either case, this book will get you up and running quickly. It would be helpful to have a bit of familiarity with basic programming concepts, but no prior experience is required.

# Conventions

In this book, you will find a number of text styles that distinguish between different kinds of information. Here are some examples of these styles and an explanation of their meaning.

Code words in text, database table names, folder names, filenames, file extensions, pathnames, dummy URLs, user input, and Twitter handles are shown as follows: "Load the `randomForest` package containing the `random forest` algorithm."

A block of code is set as follows:

```
[default]
arrayFeatures <- names(dtBank)
arrayFeatures <- arrayFeatures[arrayFeatures != 'output']
formulaAll <- paste('output', '~')
formulaAll <- paste(formulaAll, arrayFeatures[1])
for(nameFeature in arrayFeatures[-1]){
  formulaAll <- paste(formulaAll, '+', nameFeature)
}
formulaAll <- formula(formulaAll)
```

When we wish to draw your attention to a particular part of a code block, the relevant lines or items are set in bold:

```
n1 + n2
[1]  5
n1 * n2
[1]  6
```

**New terms** and **important words** are shown in bold.

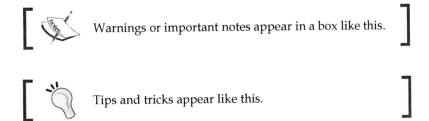

Warnings or important notes appear in a box like this.

Tips and tricks appear like this.

# Reader feedback

Feedback from our readers is always welcome. Let us know what you think about this book—what you liked or disliked. Reader feedback is important for us as it helps us develop titles that you will really get the most out of.

To send us general feedback, simply e-mail feedback@packtpub.com, and mention the book's title in the subject of your message.

If there is a topic that you have expertise in and you are interested in either writing or contributing to a book, see our author guide at www.packtpub.com/authors.

# Customer support

Now that you are the proud owner of a Packt book, we have a number of things to help you to get the most from your purchase.

## Downloading the example code

You can download the example code files from your account at `http://www.packtpub.com` for all the Packt Publishing books you have purchased. If you purchased this book elsewhere, you can visit `http://www.packtpub.com/support` and register to have the files e-mailed directly to you.

## Downloading the color images of this book

We also provide you with a PDF file that has color images of the screenshots used in this book. The color images will help you better understand the changes in the output. You can download this file from `https://www.packtpub.com/sites/default/files/downloads/7740OS_coloredimages.PDF`.

## Errata

Although we have taken every care to ensure the accuracy of our content, mistakes do happen. If you find a mistake in one of our books—maybe a mistake in the text or the code—we would be grateful if you could report this to us. By doing so, you can save other readers from frustration and help us improve subsequent versions of this book. If you find any errata, please report them by visiting `http://www.packtpub.com/submit-errata`, selecting your book, clicking on the **Errata Submission Form** link, and entering the details of your errata. Once your errata are verified, your submission will be accepted and the errata will be uploaded to our website or added to any list of existing errata under the Errata section of that title.

To view the previously submitted errata, go to `https://www.packtpub.com/books/content/support` and enter the name of the book in the search field. The required information will appear under the **Errata** section.

# Citations and references

- *Chapter 4, Step 1 – Data Exploration and Feature Engineering, Chapter 5, Step 2 – Applying Machine Learning Techniques, Chapter 6, Step 3 – Validating the Results,* and flag dataset:

  Bache, K. & Lichman, M. (2013). UCI Machine Learning Repository [http://archive.ics.uci.edu/ml]. Irvine, CA: University of California, School of Information and Computer Science.

- *Chapter 8, Machine Learning Examples Applicable to Businesses,* and bank dataset:

  [Moro et al., 2014] S. Moro, P. Cortez and P. Rita. A Data-Driven Approach to Predict the Success of Bank Telemarketing. Decision Support Systems, Elsevier, 62:22-31, June 2014

# Piracy

Piracy of copyrighted material on the Internet is an ongoing problem across all media. At Packt, we take the protection of our copyright and licenses very seriously. If you come across any illegal copies of our works in any form on the Internet, please provide us with the location address or website name immediately so that we can pursue a remedy.

Please contact us at copyright@packtpub.com with a link to the suspected pirated material.

We appreciate your help in protecting our authors and our ability to bring you valuable content.

# Questions

If you have a problem with any aspect of this book, you can contact us at questions@packtpub.com, and we will do our best to address the problem.

# 1
# Transforming Data into Actions

To face a business problem, we need the knowledge and expertise to find its solution. In addition, we also require related data that will help in identifying its solution. This chapter shows how new technologies allow us to build powerful machines that learn from data to give support to business decisions.

The topics that will be covered in this chapter are as follows:

- A general idea for approaching business problems
- The new challenges relating to digital technologies
- How the new tools help in using information
- How the tools identify the information that is not evident
- How the tools can estimate the outcome of future events
- Why R?

# A data-driven approach in business decisions

Expertise and information play important roles in business decisions. This section shows how data-driven technologies changed the approach of facing challenges and improved their solutions.

# Business decisions come from knowledge and expertise

The general idea for approaching business problems hasn't changed over the years, and it combines knowledge and information. Before using digital technologies, knowledge came from expertise provided by previous experiences and by other people. With regards to information, it was about analyzing the current situation and comparing it with past events.

A simple example is that of a fruit monger who wants to set the prices of their goods. The price of a product should maximize the profit, which depends on the sales volume and on the price itself. The dealer started their job working with their father who provided them with all their knowledge. Therefore, they already know the price of the different fruits. In addition, at the end of each day, they can observe the amount of each fruit that has been sold. Based on that, they can raise the price of fruits that sold very well and decrease the price of fruits that they didn't sell. This simple example shows how the fruit monger combines domain knowledge and information to solve their problem, as described in the following figure:

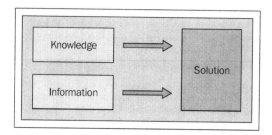

This simple example shows how a simple challenge requires a combination of knowledge and data.

# The digital era provides more data and expertise

Although the general idea for approaching business problems hasn't changed, digital technologies are providing us with new powerful tools.

The Internet allows people to connect with each other and share their expertise in such a way that everyone has access to a huge set of information. Before the Internet, knowledge came from trusted people and books. Now, the spreading of information has allowed finding books and articles written by different people from every part of the world. In addition, websites and forums allow their users to connect with each other in order to share expertise and find quick answers.

Digital technologies keep track of different activities and produce a lot of related data. We talk about data referring to sets of information—quantitative or qualitative—which is processable by machines. Therefore, when facing a business problem, we can use lots of data from different sources. Some information might not be very relevant, but even after removing it, we often have a huge amount of data. Therefore, we have a lot of improvement potential for the results.

The changes derived from digital technologies involve the process of acquiring expertise and the nature of data. Therefore, the approach to problem solving presents new challenges.

A simple example of a company that faces a business problem is a car dealer who sells different used cars and wants to set the most relevant prices. The car dealer should determine the prices based on the car model, age, and other features. This example is meant to illustrate a possible situation and is not necessarily related to a real problem.

The car dealer needs to identify the best price for each car in order to maximize the revenue. Similar to the fruit monger, if the price of a car is too high, the car dealer won't sell it in a short time, so there will be an extra storage cost and the car will lose value. This leads to an extra cost and a decrease in the profit, thereby damaging the business. On the other hand, if the price is too low, the company will sell the car immediately. Although the storage cost is lower, the company hasn't made the best profit. In order to sell cars and maximize profit, the company wants to figure out the optimal prices.

Let's take a look at the expertise and information that help in finding the solution. The company can use:

- The knowledge of agents who have already sold different cars
- Information from the Internet
- The data about previous sales

The agents can use their past experience, so their knowledge helps in identifying the best prices. However, it's not enough to set the prices when the market changes quickly.

The Internet gives us a lot of information since there are many online shopping websites displaying the prices of used cars. Online shopping is different from the physical market, but an expert agent can take a look at the websites and compare the prices. In this way, the agent can combine their expertise with the online information and identify the right prices in a good way.

This approach leads to good results, but is still not optimal. Looking at different websites is time-consuming, especially if there are many categories of cars, so it is hard or even impossible to check the prices on a daily basis. Another issue is that there might be many websites, making it impossible for a single person to process all the information. By automating our web research and using data more systematically, we can acquire information much faster.

To acquire information, the data sources are the company sales and the online market, and a good solution for car pricing should take into account all these sources. The company sales data shows how the customers reacted to their prices in the past. For instance, we know how long it took to sell each car in the past. If it took too long, the price might have been too high. This criterion is objective and an expert agent can use this information to identify the current wrong prices.

The data derived from online shopping websites displays the car prices, and we can use tools that can store a price and sales history. Although this information is less relevant to the problem, it can be processed similar to the company sales data, thereby improving the result accuracy, as described in the following figure:

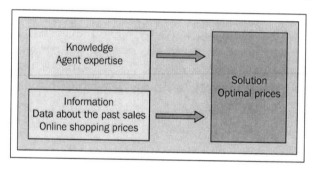

This example shows the potential of having more information and expertise. The challenge here is to use information in the most proper way to improve the solution. As a general rule, the more information we use, the more accurate the results can potentially be. In the worst case, we have a lot of irrelevant information and we can identify and use a small relevant part of it.

# Technology connects data and businesses

A single person can solve a business problem by combining data and expertise as long as the data is understandable by the human mind. The growth of data volumes due to digital technologies has changed the way of approaching problems since more data requires new tools in order to be used. In addition, new devices allow us to perform data analysis that would have been impossible on personal computers 10 years ago.

This fact not only changed the way of dealing with data, but also the overall process of making business decisions.

There are several ways to use the information contained in the data. For instance, the Internet movie streaming provider Netflix uses a tool that produces personalized movie recommendations based on your interests. **Machine learning** refers to the tools that learn from data to provide insights and actions, and it is a subfield of **artificial intelligence**. Machine learning techniques don't just process data, but rather connect data and the business. This interaction between information and knowledge is crucial and affects almost each step of building solutions.

Knowledge still plays an important role in building the tool that identifies the solution. Since there are many machine learning tools that deal with the same problem, your expertise can be used to choose the most relevant tool. In addition, most of the tools have some parameters, so it's necessary to know the problem to set them up, as described in the following figure:

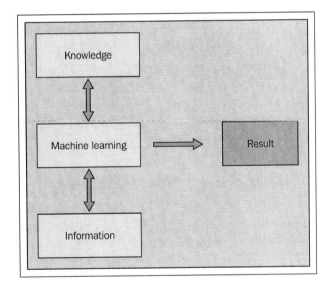

After the machine learning technique has identified a result, we can validate its performance using information and expertise. For instance, in the car dealer example, we can build a tool that automatically identifies the best prices and predict the necessary time to sell each car. Starting from the previous data, we can use the tool to estimate how long it would have taken to sell cars and compare the estimated time with the real time. In addition, we can identify the current prices and use knowledge and expertise to see if they are reasonable. In this way, we compare how similar the machine learning approach is to reality.

Validation helps in comparing different techniques and choosing the one that performs best. In addition, techniques usually need a setup with different options, and validation helps in choosing the most proper option, as described in the following figure:

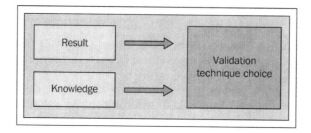

In conclusion, the interaction between machine learning and business is extremely important, and it takes place in each part of the process of building the solution.

# Identifying hidden patterns

Data displays some information that is evident and it contains a lot of other information that is more implicit. Sometimes, the solution to a business problem requires some information that is less evident and which may be partly subjective. This section shows how some machine learning techniques discover hidden structures and patterns from the data.

# Data contains hidden information

Data that tracks an activity contains the information related to a technology device. For instance, in a supermarket, the checkout machines track the purchases. Therefore, it's possible to have some information about the sales of each item in the past. The available information is the **Point of Sale** (POS) data and it displays the transactions through the following attributes:

- Item ID
- Number of units that have been sold
- Price of the item
- Date and time of the purchase
- The checkout machine's ID
- Customer ID (for customers that use a Nectar card)

Some information is manifested and is easily accessible by analyzing the data, whereas some other information is hidden. Starting from the transactions, it's easy to determine the total amount of sales in the past. For instance, we can count how many units of a product have been sold in a day. It is very easy to do so:

1.  Select the transactions based on the product ID and the day.
2.  Add the number of units.

It's still easy to obtain some slightly more elaborated information. We can divide the items into departments, and with the knowledge of the total units that have been sold in each department in the previous year, we can:

1.  Generate a list of product IDs for each department.
2.  For each department, select the transactions of the previous year and of the product IDs of the department.
3.  Add the number of units.

It's possible to extract any other kind of information about the overall sales in the past. What if the targets of the analysis are the customers instead of the sales?

We can use the customer ID in order to track the purchases of each customer. For instance, given a single customer ID, we can determine the total number of units that they purchased. This data is still easy to obtain, so we can't talk about hidden patterns. However, there is still a lot of information about the customers that cannot be directly displayed.

Some customers have similar customer habits. Examples of customer categories are:

*   Students
*   Housewives
*   Elderly people

Each group of people displays some specific purchase habits that are as follows:

*   Available money to spend
*   Products that the customers are interested in
*   Date and time of the purchase

For instance, students have, on average, less money to spend than other people. Moms are keener to buy groceries and products for the house. Students are more likely to go to the supermarket after school; elderly people will go at almost any time of day.

The data doesn't display which customer IDs are associated with each category of customers, even if it contains some information about their behavior. However, it's hard to identify which customers are similar in order to perform a simple analysis operation. In addition, in order to identify the groups, we need to have an initial guess about the categories of customers.

# Business problems require hidden information

A business problem might require some hidden information. In the supermarket example, we want to address an ad-hoc marketing and discount campaign to some groups of customers.

The options of the marketing campaign determine the following:

* Which items are advertised
* Which items are discounted
* The discount
* Which weekdays are affected by the promotion

If the supermarket was very small, it would have been possible to extract the data about each customer and consequently address them with a specific campaign. However, the supermarket is big and there are many customers, so it'll be impossible to take into account each one of them separately without the use of some data processing.

A possibility is to define a method that automatically reads the data about each customer and consequently chooses the marketing campaign. This approach requires the following:

* Organizing the data and selected information
* Modeling the data
* Defining the action

This approach works, although it has some drawbacks. The decision about a marketing campaign requires a general picture about the customer base. After having understood the patterns in the customer behavior, it's possible to define a method for the purpose of choosing the marketing campaign starting from the customer behavior. Therefore, this method requires some previous analysis.

Another solution is to identify groups of customers that have similar habits. Once the groups are defined, it's possible to analyze each group separately in order to understand its common purchase behavior.

The following chart shows some customers represented by small circles, where the big circles represent the homogeneous groups of customers:

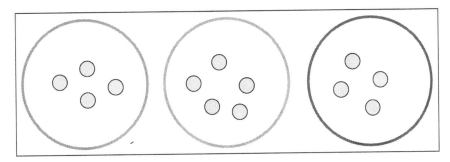

In this way, the supermarket has some information about each group that helps them identify the right marketing campaign by combining the following:

- Some aggregated information about the customers of the group
- Some business knowledge that allows them to define a proper marketing campaign

Assuming that each customer will have the same habits in the future, at least in the short term, it's possible to identify the purchase behavior and interests of each group of customers and consequently target them with the same campaign.

# Reshaping the data

Starting from the POS data, we want to model the purchase habits of the supermarket customers in order to identify homogeneous groups. Although the POS data doesn't display the customer behavior directly, it contains the customer ID. The behavior of each customer can be modeled by measuring their habits. For instance, we can measure the total number of units that they have purchased over the last few years. Similarly, we can define some other **Key Performance Indicators (KPIs)** that are values describing different aspects of the behavior. After extracting all the transactions related to a customer, we can define KPIs as follows:

- The total number of units that they purchased in the previous year
- The total amount of money that they spent in the last year

- The percentage of units that they purchased between 6 p.m. and 7 p.m.
- The total money spent in a specific item department
- The percentage of money that they spent in summer

There are different options for choosing the KPIs and they should be relevant to the problem. In our example, we want to determine in which products the customers are likely to be interested.

Some KPIs that are relevant to the problem are as follows:

- The total money spent in the last year, in order to identify the maximum amount of money that a customer can spend
- The percentage of money spent in different item departments, in order to identify what the customer is interested in
- The percentage of purchases in the morning and in the early afternoon, in order to identify housewives and pensioners

Given a small set of customers, it's easy to identify homogeneous groups by observing the data. However, if we have many customers and/or KPIs, we need computing tools to uncover the hidden patterns in the data.

# Identifying patterns with unsupervised learning

There are some machine learning algorithms that identify hidden structures, and this branch of techniques is called "unsupervised learning". Starting from the data, the unsupervised learning algorithms identify patterns and labels that are not directly displayed.

In our example, we model the customers using a proper set of KPIs that describe their purchase behavior. Our target is to identify groups that have similar values for the KPIs.

In order to associate the customers, the first step is to measure how similar they are. Observing the data of two customers, we can see that they are similar if the values of their KPIs are similar. Since there are many customers, we can't observe data manually, so we need to define a criterion. The criterion is a function that takes as an input the KPIs of two customers and computes a *distance*, which is a number that expresses the dissimilarity between the values. In this way, there is an objective way to state how *similar* two customers are.

We have modeled the customers through *objects* whose *similarity* can be measured. There are several machine learning algorithms that group *similar* objects, and they're called **clustering techniques**. The techniques group together similar customers and consequently identify homogeneous groups.

There are different options to group the customers, depending on:

- The number of desired clusters
- The relevance of each KPI
- The way to identify clusters

There are different options for clustering, and most of the algorithms contain some parameters. In order to choose the proper technique and setup, we need to explore the data to understand the business problem.

This chapter is just an introductory chapter, and clustering is just an example of unsupervised learning.

# Making business decisions with unsupervised learning

Clustering techniques allow us to identify homogeneous groups of customers. For each cluster, the supermarket has to define a marketing campaign targeting its customers using promotions and discounts.

For each cluster, it's possible to define a summary table showing the average customer's behavior. Combining this information with some business expertise, the supermarket can maximize the positive impact of the campaign.

In conclusion, clustering allows us to convert a massive volume of data into a small set of relevant information. Then, a business expert can read and understand the clustering results to make the best decisions.

This example showed how data and expertise are strongly linked. The machine learning algorithms required the KPIs that are defined using business expertise. After the algorithm has processed the data, business expertise is necessary to identify the right action.

# Estimating the impact of an action

When a business decision consists of choosing between different options, the solution requires estimating the impact of each of them. This chapter shows how machine learning techniques predict future events depending on the options, and how we can measure the accuracy.

## Business problems require estimating future events

If we have to choose between different options, we estimate the impact of each alternative and choose the best. In order to illustrate this, the example is a big supermarket that plans to start selling a new item, and the business decision consists of choosing its price.

In order to choose the best price, the company needs to know:

- The price options
- The impact of each price option on the item sales
- The impact of each price option on the sales of other items

The ideal solution is to maximize the impact of the overall revenue for the short and long term. Regarding the item itself, if its price is too high, the company won't sell it, missing a potential profit. On the other hand, if the price is too low, the company will sell different units without making good revenue.

In addition, the price of a new item will have an impact on the sales of similar items. For instance, if the supermarket is selling a new cereal, the sales of all the other cereal products will be affected. If the new price is too low, some of the customers purchasing the other items will want to save money and consequently purchase the new item. In this way, some customers will spend less money and the overall revenue will decrease. Conversely, if the new item is overpriced, the customers might perceive that the other items are too cheap and consequently that their quality is lower.

There are different effects, and one option is to define a minimum and maximum price of the item as a first step, in order to avoid negative effects on the sales of the related items. Then, we can choose the new price, maximizing the revenue of the item itself.

# Gathering the data to learn from

Let's assume that we have already defined the minimum and maximum price for the new item. The goal is to use the data in order to discover the information that allows us to maximize the revenue of the item. The revenue depends on:

- The price of the item
- The units that will be sold in the next month

In order to maximize the revenue, we want to estimate it depending on the price, and pick the price that maximizes it. If we can estimate the sales volume depending on the price, we can consequently estimate the revenue.

The data displays information of past transactions, which include:

- Item ID
- Date
- Number of units that have been sold during the day
- Price of the item

There are also other data mapping the item that include some features. In order to simplify the problem, the features are all categorical, so they display categories instead of numbers. Examples of features are as follows:

- Department
- Product
- Brand
- Other categorical features that define the item

We don't have any data about the sales of the new item, so we need to estimate the customer behavior using data about some similar items. We're assuming that:

- The future customers' behavior is similar to the past
- The customers' behavior is similar across similar items
- The sales of the new item are not affected by the fact that it's new to the market

As we want to estimate the sales volume of the new item, the starting point is the sales volume of similar items. For each item, we extract its transactions in the last month and we compute:

- The total number of units in the last month
- The most common price in the last month

In addition, for each item, we have the data defining its features. The data about each item is the starting point to estimate the revenue.

# Predicting future outcomes using supervised learning

In our problem, the target of machine learning algorithms is to forecast the sales volume of an item depending on its price. The branch of techniques that learn from the data to forecast a future event is called **supervised learning**. The starting point of the algorithms is a training set of data that consists of objects whose event is already known. The algorithms identify a relationship between the data that describes the object and the event. Then, they build a model that defines this relationship and use the model for forecasting the event on other objects. The difference between supervised and unsupervised learning is that supervised learning techniques use training with known events whereas unsupervised learning techniques identify patterns that were hidden.

For instance, we have a new item whose price can either be $2, $3, or $4. In order to have the optimal price, we need to estimate the future revenues.

The data displays the sales volume of any item depending on its price and features. The approach for estimating the sales volume of a new item, depending on its price, is to use the sales volume of a defined number ($k$) of items that are the most similar. For each price, the steps are as follows:

1. Define which are the $k$ most similar items, given the features and the price of the new item.
2. Define how to use the data of the similar items to estimate the sales volume of the new item.

In order to identify the most similar items, we have to decide what is *similar* and how *similar* it is. In order to do that, we can define a way to measure the similarity between any two items depending on the features and on the price. The similarity can be measured through a distance function, taking into account these features:

- Price difference
- Same product
- Same brand
- Same department
- Other similar features

An easy way is to measure the distance as the sum of dissimilarities between the features. For instance, a very simple dissimilarity can be the price difference plus the number of categorical features that display different values. A slightly more advantageous way is to give a different weight to each feature on the basis of its relevancy. For instance, two items that do not belong to the same department are very dissimilar, whereas two items that are of the same product but of different brands are very similar.

After defining the distance function, we want to identify the $k$ most similar objects depending on the price. For each price point, we define an item with the features of the new item and the chosen price. Then, for each item in the supermarket, we compute the distance between the item and the new item. In this way, we can pick the $k$ items whose distance is the lowest.

After having identified the $k$ most similar items, we need to determine how to use this information in order to estimate the new volume. A simple method is to compute the average between the sales volumes of the $k$ items. A more advanced approach is to give more importance to more similar items.

The techniques that estimate a future event depending on the past data are called supervised learning techniques. The algorithm that has been illustrated is the **k-nearest neighbors (KNN)** algorithm, and it's one of the most basic supervised learning techniques.

# Summary

This chapter showed how business problems are faced by combining expertise and information. You saw how digital technologies led to an increment of the volume of information and provided us with new techniques to face challenges. You had an overview about the two most important branches of machine learning techniques: unsupervised and supervised learning. Unsupervised learning techniques identify some structures that are hidden in the data and supervised learning techniques use the data for estimating an unknown situation.

The next chapter shows the challenges related to machine learning problems and defines the requirements of software that identifies their solution. Then, the chapter introduces the software that we will be using in this book and provides you with a brief tutorial.

# 2
# R – A Powerful Tool for Developing Machine Learning Algorithms

Before using the machine learning techniques, we need to choose the proper software. There are many programming languages and types of software that provide the user with machine learning tools. In fact, the most important part is knowing which techniques to use and how to build new ones, and the software is just a tool. However, choosing the right software allows you to build faster and more accurate solutions.

In this chapter, you will learn:

- The software requirements for building a machine learning solution
- How R, combined with RStudio, facilitates the development of a machine learning solution
- The structure of R
- The tools of R
- Some important R packages

## Why R

Understanding the challenges in developing machine learning solutions helps in choosing the software that allows you to face them in the easiest and most effective way. This chapter illustrates the software requirements and explains why we will use R.

# An interactive approach to machine learning

Developing a machine learning solution consists of steps that have different requirements. In addition, the result of a step helps in improving the previous, so it's often necessary to come back to modify it.

Before facing a problem and building its machine learning solution, we want to know as much as possible about the challenge and the available resources. Effectively, it's very important to have all the possible information in order to define the right path to the solution. For this purpose, starting from the data, we extract business insights and patterns from the data using statistical and machine learning tools.

A simple example is a big supermarket that launches a new marketing campaign that targets some specific customers. The available data is the transactions about the past sales. Before building any machine learning technique, we need some basic information such as the total number of customers and the total sales volume in the previous year. After knowing the total number of customers, we want to identify the average customer's annual expenditure. Then, the next step can be to divide the customers in groups with homogeneous purchasing habits and compute the average customer's annual expenditure for each group.

After extracting some basic information, we have a more detailed overview of the problem, and there will be new questions coming out very often. Therefore, we need to identify new patterns and extract new insights by applying other statistical and machine learning models. This procedure will go on until the information allows us to identify the final machine learning solution.

There are often different options for a solution to a problem. In order to choose the most proper one, we can build some of them and compare their results. In addition, most of the algorithms can be tuned to improve their performance, and the tuning depends on the results.

In conclusion, building a machine learning solution consists of different steps strongly related with each other. The target of a new step is based on the analysis of the previous one, and sometimes, a step is modified on the basis of the following results. There isn't a well-defined path that goes from the start to the end, and the software should allow that.

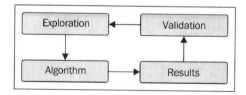

# Expectations of machine learning software

There are different options for a machine learning software, and this section shows what we are expecting from our choice. The software should, at the same time, provide the user with the machine learning tools and allow specific solutions to be built.

The most important machine learning techniques are provided by different types of software and packages. However, using cutting-edge techniques improves the solution. Most of the machine learning algorithms are developed by the academic world and used for research, so it takes time before they come into business. In addition, apart from a few exceptions, companies don't have enough resources to develop advanced techniques. Therefore, software should allow the user to access the tools developed in academia. In the case of free and open source software, there is usually an international community that provides the users with many packages that contain cutting-edge tools.

Another software requirement is to allow the user to develop quick and effective solutions. The approach to the machine learning problems requires a lot of interaction in the sense that the user often modifies the solution depending on the result. A good user-friendly graphic package is important to explore the results of each step and determine what to do. Therefore, the tool should allow the user to quickly build reusable components for data exploration, process, and visualization.

In conclusion, the software requirements are:

- Machine learning tools
- Graphic packages
- Reusability of components

# R and RStudio

The software that we will use is R and this subsection explains why.

**R** is a programming language designed for data analysis and machine learning. It's an interpreted language in the sense that it executes the commands directly, so it is more user friendly than other programming languages. Although its learning curve is steeper compared to some commercial software, R is easier to learn compared to other programming languages.

R is the most popular programming language for statistics, and there is a huge international community that supports it. Its repository (CRAN) contains more than 5,000 packages with statistics and machine learning tools. In this way, we can use the most cutting-edge tools provided by its international community.

Other useful R tools are its graphic packages that allow the generation of nice and professional charts using just a few lines of code. In this way, it's very easy to explore data and results during the solution development.

Another advantage of R is **RStudio**, which is an IDE projected for R. RStudio includes an interactive console and tools that are used to access the R help, visualize/save charts, and for debugging. R, combined with RStudio, allows the users to develop powerful machine learning solutions relatively quickly.

# The R tutorial

I assume that you are already familiar with a programming language, although not necessarily R. This section contains a brief R tutorial that shows some tools that are useful for building machine learning solutions. Since a proper introduction to R would require an entire book, this tutorial focuses on just some relevant topics.

If you're already familiar with R, you can quickly read through this section. If you're new to R, I advise you to combine this section with an interactive online tutorial to get a more complete overview. In addition, it'll be very useful to play with the tools in order to acquire more familiarity.

Before starting with the tutorial, we need to install R and RStudio. Both types of software are open source, and they support the most relevant operating systems. It's also useful to read the RStudio tutorial to understand how to use this powerful IDE.

My advice is to generate a new R script in the RStudio environment and to copy and paste the code into the script. You can run the command by going to the specific command line and pressing *Ctrl + Enter*.

# The basic tools of R

The basic structure of R is very easy. Any kind of variable is stored in an object that can be visualized by typing its name. Let's start defining some numbers:

```
n1 <- 2
n2 <- 3
```

We can visualize an object by typing its name, as follows:

```
n1
[1] 2
```

We can perform some basic operations on the objects:

```
n1 + n2
[1] 5
n1 * n2
[1] 6
```

The output of any operation can be stored in another object:

```
nSum <- n1 + n2
nProd <- n1 * n2
nSum
[1] 5
```

The standard syntax used to add comments to the code consists of starting the line with a hash, as shown:

```
# we performed some basic operations on the numbers
```

We can apply the R functions to the object and the syntax is very easy since the arguments are always within the parenthesis: `result <- functionName(argument1, argument2, ...)`.

For instance, we can use `sum` to compute the sum of numeric variables:

```
sum(2, 3)
[1] 5
sum(2, 3, 4)
[1] 9
```

Similarly, for the operators, we can store the output of a function into another object, as shown:

```
s1 <- sum(2, 3)
s2 <- sum(2, 3, 4)
```

There are also functions that print a message on the console. For instance, given any object, `print` displays its content in the same way, that is, by just typing the object name:

```
print(s1)
[1] 5
```

The syntax used to define new functions is easy. For instance, we can define a function, `funProd`, which computes the product of its two arguments:

```
funProd <- function(n1, n2)
{
  n <- n1 * n2
  return(n)
}
```

The `n1` and `n2` inputs are defined within the parenthesis and the operations are contained in the curly brackets. The `return` method terminates the function, giving the result as the output. We can visualize the code within any function just by typing its name.

In order to keep track of what the function is doing, we can print the variables while the function is executing, shown as follows:

```
funProdPrint <- function(n1, n2){
  n <- n1 * n2
  print(n1)
  print(n2)
  print(n)
  return(n)
}
prod <- funProdPrint(n1 = 2, n2 = 3)
[1]  2
[1]  3
[1]  6
```

**Downloading the example code**

You can download the example code files from your account at
`http://www.packtpub.com` for all the Packt Publishing books you
have purchased. If you purchased this book elsewhere, you can visit
`http://www.packtpub.com/support` and register to have the
files e-mailed directly to you.

There are different R functions associated with documentation. We can use `help` to display their description, as shown:

```
help(sum)
```

Another option is to use `sum`, but personally, I prefer to use `help` in order to use the same parenthesis syntax of the other R functions.

In order to perform basic R operations, we have to store the data in the vectors that are objects that contain a sorted collection of values. We can define a new vector using c, which is a function that concatenates its input, shown as follows:

```
a1 <- c(1, 2, 3)
a1
[1] 1 2 3
```

We can extract an element of the vector using square brackets. The first element can be extracted putting 1 inside the square brackets. Please note that R indexes differently from other programming languages such as Python, where the first element is indexed as 0 instead of 1, as shown here:

```
a1[1]
[1] 1
```

We can extract more than one element at the same time by putting a vector inside the square brackets, as shown here:

```
a1[c(1, 2)]
[1] 1 2
```

We can also perform some basic operations on the vectors:

```
a sPaste <- paste(s1, s2, sep = '_')
1 + 1
[1] 2 3 4
a2 <- c(1, 2, 3)
a1 + a2
[1] 2 4 6
```

If we want to define a vector that contains a sequence of integers, we can use this notation:

```
a3 <- 1:10
a3
[1]  1  2  3  4  5  6  7  8  9 10
```

The vectors can contain undefined values, which are NA in R:

```
a4 <- c(1, NA, 2)
```

If we perform an operation on an NA value, the output will be NA.

Another important data element is Boolean. Boolean variables are defined using TRUE and FALSE, and the basic operators are & or && (AND), | or || (OR), as well as ! (NOT). Boolean elements can be single elements or vectors. In the case of vectors, the shorter forms (& and |) compare each element and the long forms (&& and ||) evaluate only the first element of each vector, shown as follows:

```
bool1 <- TRUE
bool2 <- FALSE
bool3 <- bool1 & bool2
bool4 <- bool1 | bool2
bool5 <- !bool1
bool3
[1] FALSE
bool4
[1] TRUE
bool5
[1] FALSE
```

We can define Boolean variables using relational operators such as == (equal to), != (not equal to), <= (less than or equal to), >=, <, and >:

```
x1 <- 1
x2 <- 2
bool5 <- x1 == x2
bool6 <- x1 != x2
bool7 <- x1 <= x2
bool5
[1] FALSE
bool6
[1] TRUE
bool7
[1] FALSE
```

Boolean variables can be included in the if statements defined by if with a syntax similar to the functions. We put the condition within the parenthesis and the operations are within the curly brackets, shown as follows:

```
if(bool5){
  x <- 1
}else{
  x <- 2
}
x
[1] 2
```

We can define `for` loops using `for` and their syntax is the same as `if`. The parenthesis contains the variable name and the vector with the values, and the curly brackets contain the operations, shown as follows:

```
vectorI <- c(1, 2, 5)
x <- 0
for(i in vectorI)
{
  if(i > 1)
  {
    x <- x + i
  }
}
x
[1]  7
```

If we want to repeat an operation for a fixed number of times, we can define a vector that contains the first *n* integer numbers:

```
nIter <- 10
vectorIter <- 1:nIter
total <- 0
for(i in vectorIter){
  total <- total + 1
}
total
[1]  10
```

This subsection showed some basic components of R. The next subsection presents the R objects that analyze the data.

# Understanding the basic R objects

There are different kinds of objects, and we have seen some of them: `numeric`, `function`, `boolean`, and `vector`. We can easily identify the class of the objects used in the previous examples.

Consider the following example:

```
class(n1)
[1] "numeric"
class(funProd)
[1] "function"
class(bool5)
[1] "logical"
class(a1)
[1] "numeric"
```

The `a1` vector belongs to the `numeric` class because all its elements are numeric. In the same way, a vector with logical elements belongs to `logical`.

Strings are defined using single or double quotes, shown as follows:

```
s1 <- 'string1'
s2 <- "string2"
```

There are different string functions such as `paste`, which concatenates two strings, and `substring`, which extracts a subset from the string, as shown:

```
sPaste <- paste(s1, s2, sep = '_')
sPaste
[1] "string1_string2"
sSub <- substring(sPaste, 2, 5)
sSub
[1] "trin"
```

It's possible to define a `string` vector in the same way as `numeric` or `logical`:

```
vectorStrings <- c(s1, s2, sPaste, sSub)
vectorStrings
[1] "string1"         "string2"         "string1_string2" "trin"
class(vectorStrings)
[1] "character"
```

A vector can include any kind of object (even functions potentially). What happens if we define a vector that contains strings and numbers?

```
vectorStringsNum <- c(s1, s2, 10, 1.3)
vectorStringsNum
[1] "string1" "string2" "10"      "1.3"
class(vectorStringsNum)
[1] "character"
```

As shown in the preceding code, R converted the numbers into characters in order to have a homogeneous vector. However, there are other data structures that allow us to store heterogeneous objects.

If we have categoric variables, we can use strings to store them, but there is another option: `factors`. This R object contains a variable whose value belongs to a defined set of values known as `levels`. Each level is associated with an integer and the data can be treated as integers or characters that obtain the same result. Factors can also help in creating ordinal variables.

Starting from a string, we can generate a factor using `factor`:

```
vectorString <- c('a', 'a', 'b', 'c')
vectorFactor <- factor(vectorString)
class(vectorFactor)
[1] "factor"
```

Using levels, we can identify the possible values:

```
levels(vectorFactor)
```

Another useful function, although not necessarily related to factors, is `table`, and it counts the occurrences of each level:

```
table(vectorFactor)
vectorFactor
a b c
2 1 1
```

Another useful data element is `Date`, and it is one of the R options used to store dates. We start building a string such as `'2013-01-01'` and defining the position of the year, month, and day in another string, as shown:

```
stringDate <- '2013-01-01'
formatDate <- '%Y-%m-%d'
```

Now, using `as.Date`, we can generate the date object:

```
date1 <- as.Date(stringDate, format = formatDate)
class(date1)
[1] "Date"
date1
[1] "2013-01-01"
```

We can apply simple operations on dates, such as adding a definite number of days:

```
date2 <- date1 + 10
date2
[1] "2013-01-11"
```

We can also use Boolean operators to match two dates:

```
date1 > date2
[1] FALSE
```

Another data type is `list`, and it defines an ordered heterogeneous collection of data elements:

```
l1 <- list(1, a1, sPaste)
l1
[[1]]
[1] 1

[[2]]
[1] 1 2 3

[[3]]
[1] "string1_string2"
```

Each object can be associated with a key that allows us to access it:

```
l2 <- list(elNumber = 1, elvector = a1, elString = sPaste)
l2
$elNumber
[1] 1

$elVector
[1] 1 2 3

$elString
[1] "string1_string2"
```

In both cases, we can extract an element from a list using a double square bracket and the position of the element, as shown:

```
l1[[1]]
[1] 1
l2[[1]]
[1] 1
```

In the case of `l2`, we have defined its key, so we can access its elements using the `$` operator:

```
l2$elNumber
[1] 1
```

We can visualize all the key names using `names`:

```
names(l2)
[1] "elNumber" "elVector"  "elString"
```

It's also possible to define or change the key names:

```
names(l1) <- c('el1', 'el2', 'el3')
names(l1)
[1] "el1" "el2" "el3"
```

In order to extract a sublist from a list, we can use the single square brackets, similar to the vectors:

```
l3 <- l2[1]
l3
$elNumber
[1] 1
l4 <- l2[c(1, 2)]
l4
$elNumber
[1] 1


$elVector
[1] 1 2 3
```

An R object that allows you to store tabular data is a `matrix`. To generate a new matrix, put all the values in a vector and use `matrix`, shown as follows:

```
vectorMatrix <- c(1, 2, 3, 11, 12, 13)
matrix1 <- matrix(vectorMatrix, ncol = 2)
matrix1
     [,1] [,2]
[1,]    1   11
[2,]    2   12
[3,]    3   13
```

Using `t`, we can transpose a matrix, which means we can switch the rows with the columns:

```
matrix2 <- t(matrix1)
matrix2
     [,1] [,2] [,3]
[1,]    1    2    3
[2,]   11   12   13
```

As shown in the preceding code, `matrix1` and `matrix2` contain only numeric data. Using `cbind`, we can add another column. What happens if we add a character column?

```
vector3 <- c('a', 'b', 'c')
matrix3 <- cbind(matrix1, vector3)
matrix3
```

R converts numbers into characters. The reason is that the matrices, like vectors, can contain only homogeneous data.

The matrices can have row and column names, and we can display them using `rownames` and `colnames`:

```
rownames(matrix3)
NULL
colnames(matrix3)
[1] ""          ""          "vector3"
```

We defined `matrix3` by adding a column to `matrix3`. Its columns and R automatically set the last column name equal to the vector name, that is, `vector3`. Using the same functions, we can set the row and column names manually, as shown:

```
rownames(matrix3) <- c('row1', 'row2', 'row3')
colnames(matrix3) <- c('col1', 'col2', 'col3')
matrix3
     col1 col2 col3
row1 "1"  "11" "a"
row2 "2"  "12" "b"
row3 "3"  "13" "c"
```

We can visualize a data frame using `View`:

```
View(df2)
```

> For the data frames, refer to the scripts of this chapter.

There are some functions that allow the same operation to be performed on each element of a vector, matrix, or list. The functions are as follows:

- `apply`: Apply a function to each row, column, or element of a matrix
- `sapply`: Apply a function to each element of a vector
- `lapply`: Apply a function to each element of a list

The `sapply` function is the easiest, so we can start with it. We can define a vector `x1` with the integer numbers between `1` and `10`, and a function, `func1`, which returns the square of the input:

```
x1 <- 1:10
func1 <- function(el){
  result <- el ^ 2
  return(result)
}
```

Now, we can use `sapply` by specifying the arguments: `X`—the array, and `FUN`—the function:

```
sapply(X = x1, FUN = func1)
 [1]    1    4    9   16   25   36   49   64   81  100
```

Similarly, we can use `lapply`:

```
l1 <- list(a = 1, b = 2, c = 3)
lapply(X = l1, FUN = func1)
$a
[1] 1

$b
[1] 4

$c
[1] 9
```

The function that performs an operation on a matrix is `apply`. It can be used to apply the same function to each row. Let's first define a matrix:

```
matrix4 <- matrix(1:9, nrow = 3)
matrix4
     [,1] [,2] [,3]
[1,]    1    4    7
[2,]    2    5    8
[3,]    3    6    9
```

In order to apply the `sum` function to each row, we use `apply`, defining the `MARGIN` input equal to `1`, which specifies that we perform the operation on each row:

```
apply(X = matrix4, MARGIN = 1, FUN = sum)
[1] 12 15 18
```

Defining `MARGIN = 2`, we perform the operation on each column:

```
apply(X = matrix4, MARGIN = 2, FUN = sum)
[1]   6 15 24
```

We can apply the function to each element of the matrix using `MARGIN = c(1, 2)`:

```
apply(X = matrix4, MARGIN = c(1, 2), FUN = func1)
     [,1] [,2] [,3]
[1,]    1   16   49
[2,]    4   25   64
[3,]    9   36   81
```

This section showed some R objects and tools that are relevant to machine learning analysis. However, they're still just the basics.

# What are the R standards?

There are some style rules for having a clean and standardized code, and this subsection shows some of them.

Unlike other programming languages, R doesn't require any indentation. However, indenting the code makes it more readable and clean. The R standard is to use two spaces, and RStudio automatically defines this indentation.

The standard for assigning a variable is to use the `<-` operator even if it's possible to use `=` to make R more similar to other programming languages. However, the two operators have a different meaning if used within function input.

There are different options for the identifiers, and personally, I like the lower camel case:

```
lowerCamelCase
```

However, the R community is very big and there are different conventions.

Each operator should be surrounded by spaces, and in a function's input, there should always be a space after a comma:

```
x <- 1
sum(1, 2)
```

There are some other style rules, and you can find them at `https://google-styleguide.googlecode.com/svn/trunk/Rguide.xml`.

# Some useful R packages

There are different R packages that provide users with general-purpose functions and specific techniques. This chapter introduces two powerful general purpose packages: `data.table` and `plyr`.

Some packages are already installed in the basic version of R. However, in order to use `data.table` and `plyr`, we need to download them from the official CRAN repository using `install.packages`. Let's start with `data.table`, which is a package that provides additional tools used to deal with data frames:

```
install.packages('data.table')
```

If the command doesn't work, you can specify the repository:

```
install.packages(
  pkgs = 'data.table',
  repos = 'http://cran.us.r-project.org'
)
```

After installing the package, we need to load it in order to use its functions. Unfortunately, R will import all the functions from the package without using a namespace, and sometimes there might be name conflicts across different packages:

```
library(data.table)
```

The package contains a new class called `data.table`, which inherits from `data.frame`. Inheritance means that data tables can use all the data frame tools, if not overrided, plus others.

In order to use the package, the starting point is a dataset that we will analyze. R provides the user with some datasets, and we can see their list and description using `data`:

```
data()
```

The dataset that we will use is `iris`. Although it's a very standard dataset for the tutorials, I decided to use it since it's good to use to show the data table tools. I promise that I will choose more interesting topics in the following chapters. First, let's read the data description:

```
help(iris)
```

The dataset contains the data about three species of iris flowers: `setosa`, `versicolor`, and `virginica`. The data displays the length and the width of the sepal and the petals of each flower.

The `iris` dataset is a data frame. First, let's convert it into a data table using `data.table`:

```
class(iris)
[1] "data.frame"
dtIris <- data.table(iris)
class(dtIris)
[1] "data.table" "data.frame"
```

The `dtIris` object belongs to the `data.table` and `data.frame` classes because of inheritance. Before analyzing the data, we can use `str` to quickly explore the structure:

```
str(dtIris)
Classes 'data.table' and 'data.frame':  150 obs. of  5 variables:
 $ Sepal.Length: num  5.1 4.9 4.7 4.6 5 5.4 4.6 5 4.4 4.9 ...
 $ Sepal.Width : num  3.5 3 3.2 3.1 3.6 3.9 3.4 3.4 2.9 3.1 ...
 $ Petal.Length: num  1.4 1.4 1.3 1.5 1.4 1.7 1.4 1.5 1.4 1.5 ...
 $ Petal.Width : num  0.2 0.2 0.2 0.2 0.2 0.4 0.3 0.2 0.2 0.1 ...
 $ Species     : Factor w/ 3 levels "setosa","versicolor",..: 1 1 1 1
   1 1 1 1 1 1 ...
 - attr(*, ".internal.selfref")=<externalptr>
```

As we can see, there are four numerical columns that show the attributes of the flower and one factor column that shows the species. Now, using `print`, we can display the data contained in `dtIris`:

```
print(dtIris)
     Sepal.Length Sepal.Width Petal.Length Petal.Width   Species
  1:          5.1         3.5          1.4         0.2    setosa
  2:          4.9         3.0          1.4         0.2    setosa
  3:          4.7         3.2          1.3         0.2    setosa
  4:          4.6         3.1          1.5         0.2    setosa
  5:          5.0         3.6          1.4         0.2    setosa
 ---
146:          6.7         3.0          5.2         2.3 virginica
147:          6.3         2.5          5.0         1.9 virginica
148:          6.5         3.0          5.2         2.0 virginica
149:          6.2         3.4          5.4         2.3 virginica
150:          5.9         3.0          5.1         1.8 virginica
```

Now, we can see the first and last five rows. In order to see the whole table, we can use `View`:

```
View(dtIris)
```

After viewing the data, let's see the basic operations. The square brackets allow us to perform a wide range of operations. For instance, by putting a number in the square brackets, we extract the related row:

```
dtIris[1]
     Sepal.Length Sepal.Width Petal.Length Petal.Width Species
1:            5.1         3.5          1.4         0.2  setosa
```

By putting a vector, we can extract more rows:

```
dtIris[1:3]
     Sepal.Length Sepal.Width Petal.Length Petal.Width Species
1:            5.1         3.5          1.4         0.2  setosa
2:            4.9         3.0          1.4         0.2  setosa
3:            4.7         3.2          1.3         0.2  setosa
```

If we want to extract a column, we insert the column name as the second argument:

```
dtIris[, Species]
[1] setosa      setosa      setosa      setosa      setosa      setosa
...
[145] virginica  virginica  virginica  virginica  virginica  virginica
Levels: setosa versicolor virginica
```

Instead of the column name, we could have used the number of the column position, which, is 5 in this case. We can also extract rows and columns at the same time:

```
dtIris[1:3, Species]
[1] setosa setosa setosa
Levels: setosa versicolor virginica
```

What if we want to define a data table that has only the first three columns? We can use a similar notation, including Species as a string and adding with = F as the third argument:

```
dtIris[1:3, 'Species', with = F]
     Species
1:   setosa
2:   setosa
3:   setosa
```

We can also extract a data table with two or more columns of dtIris:

```
dtIris[1:3, c(5, 1, 2), with = F]
     Species Sepal.Length Sepal.Width
1:   setosa           5.1         3.5
2:   setosa           4.9         3.0
3:   setosa           4.7         3.2
```

We put a vector in the first argument to select rows. Like data frames and matrices, we can select the rows that define a logical vector, for instance `dtIris$Sepal.Length > 7`. In the case of data tables, we can directly access the columns without using the `$` operator. Then, we just need to include `Sepal.Length > 7` as the first argument:

```
dtIris[Sepal.Length > 7]
```

|     | Sepal.Length | Sepal.Width | Petal.Length | Petal.Width | Species   |
|-----|--------------|-------------|--------------|-------------|-----------|
| 1:  | 7.1          | 3.0         | 5.9          | 2.1         | virginica |
| 2:  | 7.6          | 3.0         | 6.6          | 2.1         | virginica |
| 3:  | 7.3          | 2.9         | 6.3          | 1.8         | virginica |
| 4:  | 7.2          | 3.6         | 6.1          | 2.5         | virginica |
| 5:  | 7.7          | 3.8         | 6.7          | 2.2         | virginica |
| 6:  | 7.7          | 2.6         | 6.9          | 2.3         | virginica |
| 7:  | 7.7          | 2.8         | 6.7          | 2.0         | virginica |
| 8:  | 7.2          | 3.2         | 6.0          | 1.8         | virginica |
| 9:  | 7.2          | 3.0         | 5.8          | 1.6         | virginica |
| 10: | 7.4          | 2.8         | 6.1          | 1.9         | virginica |
| 11: | 7.9          | 3.8         | 6.4          | 2.0         | virginica |
| 12: | 7.7          | 3.0         | 6.1          | 2.3         | virginica |

To define a new column, we can use the `:=` operator in the second square bracket argument. We can access the other columns just by typing their name. For instance, we can define `Sepal.Area` as the product of `Sepal.Length * Sepal.Width`:

```
dtIris[, Sepal.Area := Sepal.Length * Sepal.Width]
dtIris[1:6]
```

|     | Sepal.Length | Sepal.Width | Petal.Length | Petal.Width | Species | Sepal.Area |
|-----|--------------|-------------|--------------|-------------|---------|------------|
| 1:  | 5.1          | 3.5         | 1.4          | 0.2         | setosa  | 17.85      |
| 2:  | 4.9          | 3.0         | 1.4          | 0.2         | setosa  | 14.70      |
| 3:  | 4.7          | 3.2         | 1.3          | 0.2         | setosa  | 15.04      |
| 4:  | 4.6          | 3.1         | 1.5          | 0.2         | setosa  | 14.26      |
| 5:  | 5.0          | 3.6         | 1.4          | 0.2         | setosa  | 18.00      |
| 6:  | 5.4          | 3.9         | 1.7          | 0.4         | setosa  | 21.06      |

If we want to compute the average `Sepal.Area`, we can perform the operation within the second argument in the square brackets:

```
dtIris[, mean(Sepal.Area)]
[1] 17.82287
```

What if we want to know the average petal area for each species? The syntax is the same; we include `by = 'Species'` in the third argument:

```
dtIris[, mean(Sepal.Area), by = 'Species']
        Species       V1
1:       setosa 17.2578
2:   versicolor 16.5262
3:    virginica 19.6846
```

We compute more statistics at the same time. For instance, we can determine the maximum and minimum sepal area for each species. In this case, the syntax is similar, with the addition of `list` in the second argument:

```
dtIris[
    , list(areaMin = min(Sepal.Area), areaMax = max(Sepal.Area)),
    by = 'Species'
    ]
        Species areaMin areaMax
1:       setosa   10.35   25.08
2:   versicolor   10.00   22.40
3:    virginica   12.25   30.02
```

Another useful package is `plyr`, and it contains some functions similar to `apply` and is applicable in different contexts. Let's first install and load the package:

```
install.packages('plyr')
library('plyr')
```

A useful function is `dlply`, and it splits a data frame into chunks, applies a function to each chunk, and defines a list that contains the function output. The types of input are given as follows:

- `.data`: This is the data frame.
- `.variables`: This is the variable that defines the split. Each chunk corresponds to a possible value of the variable.
- `.fun`: This is the function to apply to each chunk.

For instance, starting from the `iris` data frame, we can compute the average sepal length for each species. First, we can define `funcD1` by computing the average sepal length:

```
funcD1 <- function(dtChunk){
  result <- mean(dtIris$Sepal.Length)
  return(result)
}
```

Now, we can use `dlply` to apply `funcD1` to each species:

```
dlply(
  .data = iris,
  .variables = 'Species',
  .fun = funcD1
)
$setosa
[1] 5.843333

$versicolor
[1] 5.843333

$virginica
[1] 5.843333
```

Let's explore the data that is contained in the list:

```
names(listIris)
```

Each element of the list has the name of the corresponding species. Let's take a look at one of the elements:

```
listIris$setosa
```

The `dlply` function generates a list starting from a data frame, and in the name, d stands for data frame, and l stands for list. There are other `ply` functions and the options are:

- a: Array
- d: Data frame
- l: List

For instance, `adply` defines a data frame starting from an array, and `laply` defines an array starting from a list.

This section introduced two useful packages. There are more than 5,000 packages in the CRAN repository, and we will see a few of them in the following chapters.

# Summary

In this chapter, you understood the software required to develop a machine learning solution. You saw why R, combined with RStudio, is a good tool to use to help you overcome machine learning challenges.

You learned about the basics of R and some of the most important data types and functions. You have also seen packages such as `data.table` and `plyr`.

The next chapter shows you a simple example of a challenge that can be faced using exploratory data analysis and machine learning. You will see R tools used to build charts and use machine learning algorithms.

# 3
# A Simple Machine Learning Analysis

This chapter shows examples of exploratory data analysis and machine learning techniques. R provides us with different datasets that can be used to experiment with the tools. In this chapter, we will use an interesting dataset about the Titanic passengers.

There are some facts that happened during the Titanic event, such as the policy of saving the women and children first and the privileges of the first social classes. In order to investigate what happened, we can use the data related to the event. The R dataset is about some passengers and it displays their personal data and who survived. First, we can explore some data in order to understand what happened. Then, starting from the personal data of other passengers, the goal of the machine learning model is forecasting which new passengers will survive.

In this chapter, we'll cover the following topics:

- Exploring the data
- Visualizing the data using simple charts
- Exploring the data using machine learning techniques
- Predicting an outcome using machine learning techniques

# Exploring data interactively

This section shows you how to visualize the data using simple techniques. We process the data using the `data.table` package and visualize the information using the basic R charts. A great plotting package is `ggplot2` and it allows you to create nice professional charts. Unfortunately, its syntax is more complex than the basic R charts, so we don't have enough space for it in this book.

R provides us with a `Titanic` dataset that contains the survival statistics of some passengers. Before starting to analyze the data, let's take a look at their documentation using the following code:

```
help(Titanic)
```

The documentation shows that the passengers are divided in groups on the basis of their social class, gender, and age. For each group, the dataset shows how many people survived and how many didn't. We can see the format of data using `class`:

```
class(Titanic)
[1] "table"
```

The object, `Titanic`, belongs to the `table` class so it displays the count of each combination of categoric variables, as shown:

```
Titanic
, , Age = Child, Survived = No

        Sex
Class   Male Female
   1st    0      0
   2nd    0      0
   3rd   35     17
  Crew    0      0
...
```

The table shows the frequency, that is, the number of passengers for each combination of variables that are the personal data and the data of those who survived.

# Defining a table with the data

In this subsection, we will convert the data in a more convenient format. The first step is to define a data frame:

```
dfTitanic <- data.frame(Titanic)
```

We can see the structure of dfTitanic using str:

```
str(dfTitanic)
'data.frame':    32 obs. of  5 variables:
 $ Class   : Factor w/ 4 levels "1st","2nd","3rd",..: 1 2 3 4 1 2 3 4
1 2 ...
 $ Sex     : Factor w/ 2 levels "Male","Female": 1 1 1 1 2 2 2 2 1 1
...
 $ Age     : Factor w/ 2 levels "Child","Adult": 1 1 1 1 1 1 1 1 2 2
...
 $ Survived: Factor w/ 2 levels "No","Yes": 1 1 1 1 1 1 1 1 1 1 ...
 $ Freq    : num  0 0 35 0 0 0 17 0 118 154 ...
```

There are four factors representing the passenger's attributes and Freq displaying the number of passengers for each combination of attributes. In order to use powerful tools to process data, we transform dfTitanic into a data table:

```
library(data.table)
dtTitanic <- data.table(dfTitanic)
```

We can visualize the top rows of the table using head:

```
head(dtTitanic)
     Class    Sex   Age Survived Freq
1:     1st   Male Child       No    0
2:     2nd   Male Child       No    0
3:     3rd   Male Child       No   35
4:    Crew   Male Child       No    0
5:     1st Female Child       No    0
6:     2nd Female Child       No    0
```

Here, Class, Sex, Age, and Survived represent the attributes and Freq shows the number of passengers for each combination. For instance, there are 35 male third class children that survived. The other five feature combinations having no passengers.

To start the analysis, we can define `nTot` containing the total number of passengers:

```
nTot <- dtTitanic[, sum(Freq)]
nTot
[1] 2201
```

There are `2201` passengers. Out of them, how many survived? We can use a simple data table aggregation to count the passengers that survived and the ones that didn't. We need to specify the following:

- **Operation**: In order to count the passengers, we sum up the `Freq` column, so the operation is `n=sum(Freq)`
- **Aggregation**: We count the passengers for each possible value of the `Survived` column, so we need to specify that we aggregate by `Survived`

This is the data table syntax. We use the square brackets and the three arguments are:

- **Rows to select**: We are using all the tables, so the argument is empty
- **Operations**: This contains a list containing the operation, that is, `n=sum(Freq)`
- **Aggregation**: We specify that we aggregate `by='Survived'`

Consider the following code:

```
dtSurvived <- dtTitanic[, list(n=sum(Freq)), by='Survived']
dtSurvived
    Survived    n
1:        No 1490
2:       Yes  711
```

# Visualizing the data through a histogram

We can visualize `dtSurvived` by building a histogram and the R function is `barplot`:

```
help(barplot)
```

In our case, the arguments that we need are `height` and `names.arg`, specifying the height and labels of the bars. Both the arguments require a vector in our case. Let's see how we can build the chart. Follow these steps:

1. Define the vector with height containing the number of passengers:

   ```
   vectorHeight <- dtSurvived[, n]
   ```

2. Define the vector with names containing the number of passengers that survived:

```
vectorNames <- dtSurvived[, Survived]
```

3. Build the chart:

```
barplot(height=vectorHeight, names.arg=vectorNames)
```

The histogram is as follows:

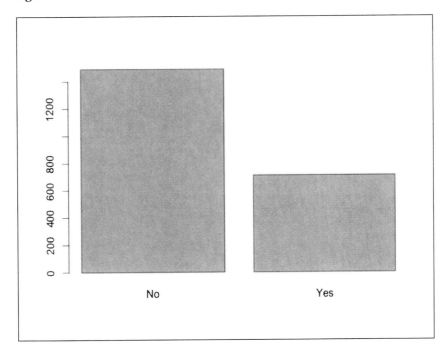

The histogram shows the number of passengers that survived or not. The height of each bar is equal to the number of passengers and the labels show what the bars represent. We could have built the same chart using just one line of code:

```
barplot(height=dtSurvived[, n], names.arg=dtSurvived[, Survived])
```

This chart shows the total number of passengers. What if we want to visualize the percentage instead? Let's take a look at the following steps:

1. Define the `percentage` column containing the number of passengers divided by the total number of passengers. We can define the new column using the `:=` data table operation. This column will be the `height` argument:

```
dtSurvived[, percentage := n / sum(n)]
```

2. Define the `colorPlot` column containing the colors blue and red for visualization. We use `ifelse` that is a function specifying that the color is blue if `Survived == 'Yes'`, and `red` otherwise. This column will be the `col` argument:

```
dtSurvived[, colorPlot := ifelse(Survived == 'Yes', 'blue',
'red')]
```

3. Build the chart and as anticipated, we include the `col` argument, defining the `color` vector. In addition, the percentage ranges between 0 and 1, so we can specify that the area of the plot will be between 0 and 1 adding the `ylim` argument equal to `c(0, 1)`:

```
barplot(
  height=dtSurvived[, percentage],
  names.arg=dtSurvived[, Survived],
  col=dtSurvived[, colorPlot],
  ylim=c(0, 1)
)
```

The histogram is as follows:

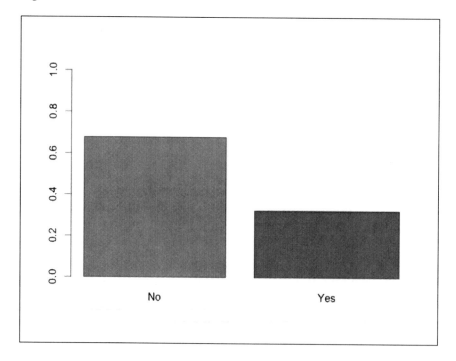

We can add a title and a legend to the chart; follow these steps:

1. Define the `textPercentage` column containing the percentage as a string. For instance, for a percentage of 0.323035, we display 32 percent in the legend:

```
dtSurvived[, textPercentage := paste(round(percentage * 100), '%',
sep='')]
```

2. Define the plot title:

```
plotTitle <- 'Proportion of passengers surviving or not'
```

3. Define the *y* axis label:

```
ylabel <- 'percentage'
```

4. Build the plot:

```
barplot(
  height=dtSurvived[, percentage],
  names.arg=dtSurvived[, Survived],
  col=dtSurvived[, colorPlot],
  ylim=c(0, 1),
  legend.text=dtSurvived[, textPercentage],
  ylab=ylabel,
  main=plotTitle
)
```

The histogram is as follows:

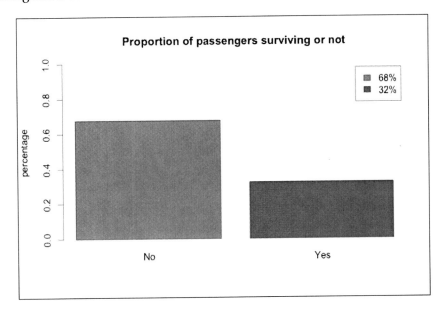

The general survival rate is **32%**, although it varies across different attribute combinations. The next subsection shows you how to visualize the impact of an attribute.

# Visualizing the impact of a feature

In this subsection, we identify the impact of gender on the survival rate. First, we can define `dtGender` displaying the number of passengers that survived or did not survive, for each gender. The operation is `n=sum(Freq)` and it is performed for each combination of `Survived` and `Sex`. Similar to the previous section, we perform a simple data table aggregation, specifying the following:

- **Rows to select**: We are using the entire table, so the argument is empty
- **Operations**: This is a list containing the operation, that is, `n=sum(Freq)`
- **Aggregation**: We aggregate by two columns, so we define `by=c('Survived', 'Sex')`

Consider the following code:

```
dtGender <- dtTitanic[, list(n=sum(Freq)), by=c('Survived', 'Sex')]
dtGender
     Survived    Sex     n
1:         No    Male 1364
2:         No  Female  126
3:        Yes    Male  367
4:        Yes  Female  344
```

Now, we can visualize the new data table through a histogram, as we saw earlier. The steps are as follows:

1. Add the `percentage` column dividing n by the number of passengers of the gender. The operation is `n / sum(n)` and it is done by gender. Then, we use the `:=` operation specifying that we compute the sum `by='Sex'`:
   ```
   dtGender[, percentage := n / sum(n), by='Sex']
   ```

2. Define the plot colors:
   ```
   dtGender[, colorPlot := ifelse(Survived == 'Yes', 'blue', 'red')]
   ```

3. Define the *y* axis label:
   ```
   dtGender[, textPercentage := paste(round(percentage * 100), '%',
   sep='')]
   ```

4. Extract the table with the male survival statistics:
   ```
   dtGenderMale <- dtGender[Sex == 'Male']
   ```

5. Build the histogram for males:

```
barplot(
  height=dtGenderMale[, percentage],
  names.arg=dtGenderMale[, Survived],
  col=dtGenderMale[, colorPlot],
  ylim=c(0, 1),
  legend.text=dtGenderMale[, textPercentage],
  ylab='percentage',
  main='Survival rate for the males'
)
```

6. Instead of extracting dtGenderMale, we could have directly built the chart adding Sex == 'Male' when extracting the vectors. We can build the same histogram for females in a similar way:

```
barplot(
  height=dtGender[Sex == 'Female', percentage],
  names.arg=dtGender[Sex == 'Female', Survived],
  col=dtGender[Sex == 'Female', colorPlot],
  ylim=c(0, 1),
  legend.text=dtGender[Sex == 'Female', textPercentage],
  ylab='percentage',
  main='Survival rate for the females'
)
```

Let's display the charts that we built:

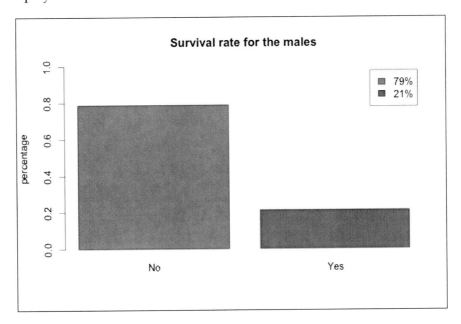

The male survival rate is just **21**% compared with 32% of passengers who survived.

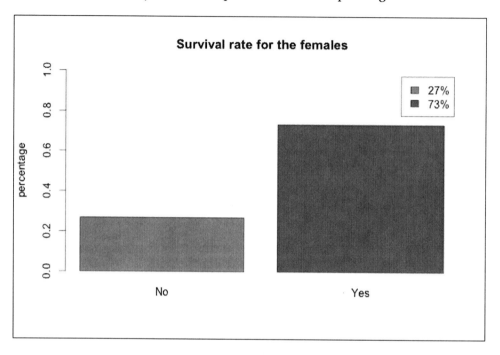

As expected, the female survival rate is significantly higher than the average.

We can compare the two genders in the same chart displaying just the survival rate that is the `Yes` column. We can build the plot using the same commands and including the `Survived == 'Yes'` condition. The only difference is the `col` argument, that in this case is the `Sex` column that is a factor with two levels. In this case, `barplot` automatically defines two colors that are black and red:

```
barplot(
  height=dtGender[Survived == 'Yes', percentage],
  names.arg=dtGender[Survived == 'Yes', Sex],
  col=dtGender[Survived == 'Yes', Sex],
  ylim=c(0, 1),
  legend.text=dtGender[Survived == 'Yes', textPercentage],
  ylab='percentage',
  main='Survival rate by gender'
)
```

The histogram is shown as follows:

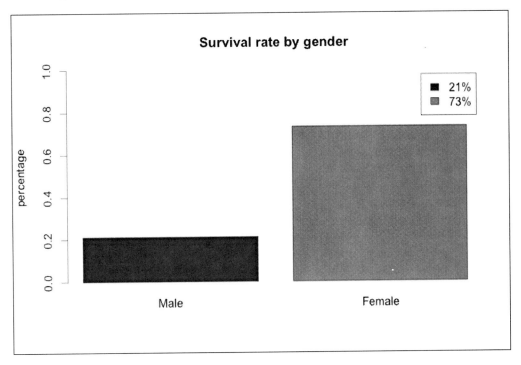

The chart allows us to visualize the difference and the legend displays the survival rate. As expected, the difference is huge.

# Visualizing the impact of two features combined

In this chapter, we investigate the impact of another feature: class. How does the survival rate vary across the different classes of passengers? First, we can just build the same survival rate chart as the one for gender, by following these steps:

1.  Define dtClass containing the passengers that survived or didn't survive for each class:

    ```
    dtClass <- dtTitanic[, list(n=sum(Freq)), by=c('Survived',
    'Class')]
    ```

2. Define the percentage of passengers that survived or didn't survive for each class:

```
dtClass[, percentage := n / sum(n), by='Class']
```

3. Define the percentage text:

```
dtClass[, textPercentage := paste(round(percentage * 100), '%',
sep='')]
```

4. Build the histogram:

```
barplot(
    height=dtClass[Survived == 'Yes', percentage],
    names.arg=dtClass[Survived == 'Yes', Class],
    col=dtClass[Survived == 'Yes', Class],
    ylim=c(0, 1),
    legend.text=dtClass[Survived == 'Yes', textPercentage],
    ylab='survival rate',
    main='Survival rate by class'
)
```

The histogram is as follows:

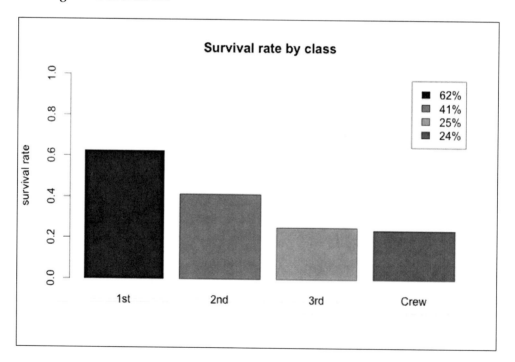

The survival rate varies a lot across the classes. We can notice that the passengers belonging to higher classes are more likely to survive and that the crew has a survival rate similar to the third class. Can we conclude that class has a high impact on the survival rate?

The chart shows the overall survival rate for each class. However, knowing that the females are more likely to survive, a class with a higher female:male ratio will likely have a higher survival rate. If a higher survival rate is explained by the gender only, the fact of belonging to a different class doesn't have an impact at all.

In order to understand whether the difference between the survival rates depends on the percentage of females in each class, we can visualize the gender ratio by class. The chart is a histogram showing the percentage of females for each social class and the commands are similar as earlier:

```
dtGenderFreq <- dtTitanic[, list(n=sum(Freq)), by=c('Sex', 'Class')]
dtGenderFreq[, percentage := n / sum(n), by='Class']
dtGenderFreq <- dtGenderFreq[Sex == 'Female']
dtGenderFreq[, textPercentage := paste(round(percentage * 100), '%',
sep='')]
barplot(
  height=dtGenderFreq[, percentage],
  names.arg=dtGenderFreq[, Class],
  col=dtGenderFreq[, Class],
  ylim=c(0, 1),
  legend.text=dtGenderFreq[, textPercentage],
  ylab='survival rate',
  main='Percentage of females'
)
```

The histogram is as follows:

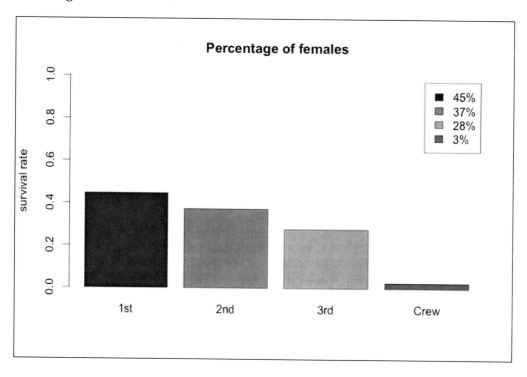

The gender ratio varies a lot across the different classes as the percentage of females is higher in the top classes, and that there are almost no females in the crew. Therefore, the percentage of females might have biased the survival rate by class. In order to have a better understanding of the impact of the two attributes on the survival rate, we need to take account of the gender and of the class at the same time. For this purpose, we can compute the survival rate for each combination of these two features. Use the following steps to build the chart:

1. Compute the sum of the passengers for each combination of `Survived`, `Sex`, and `Class`. Now the `by` argument includes three column names:

   ```
   dtGenderClass <- dtTitanic[, list(n=sum(Freq)), by=c('Survived',
   'Sex', 'Class')]
   ```

2. Add the `nTot` column specifying the total number of passengers for each feature combination (not including `Survived`). The `by` argument includes two features:

   ```
   dtGenderClass[, nTot := sum(n), by=c('Sex', 'Class')]
   ```

3. Add the `percentage` column. The `by` argument includes the two features:

```
dtGenderClass[, percentage := n / sum(n), by=c('Sex', 'Class')]
```

4. Extract the column containing the survival rate using the `Survived ==` `'Yes'` condition:

```
dtGenderClass <- dtGenderClass[Survived == 'Yes']
```

5. Add the `textPercentage` column:

```
dtGenderClass[, textPercentage := paste(round(percentage * 100),
'%', sep='')]
```

6. Add the `colorPlot` column. The `rainbow` function builds a vector with a defined number of rainbow colors. In this case, we define a column for each row, so we use `rainbow(nrow(dtGenderClass))`:

```
dtGenderClass[, colorPlot := rainbow(nrow(dtGenderClass))]
```

7. Define the group name to be included in the labels. Since the histogram will display the survival rate for each combination of both the features, we set the name of each group as the gender and the class combined, using `paste`. In order to fit the names into the chart, we define `SexAbbr` containing an abbreviation of the gender:

```
dtGenderClass[, SexAbbr := ifelse(Sex == 'Male', 'M', 'F')]
dtGenderClass[, barName := paste(Class, SexAbbr, sep='')]
```

8. Define the labels containing the plot name and the number of passengers in the group. Since we want to display the name and number in two different lines, we separate them with \n that defines a new line in a string:

```
dtGenderClass[, barLabel := paste(barName, nTot, sep='\n')]
```

9. Generate the histogram. Similar to `ylim`, the `xlim` argument defines the *x* region to visualize. In this case, we use `xlim` to avoid overlapping the legend and the chart:

```
barplot(
  height=dtGenderClass[, percentage],
  names.arg=dtGenderClass[, barLabel],
  col=dtGenderClass[, colorPlot],
  xlim=c(0, 11),
  ylim=c(0, 1),
  ylab='survival rate',
  legend.text=dtGenderClass[, textPercentage]
)
```

The histogram generated is as follows:

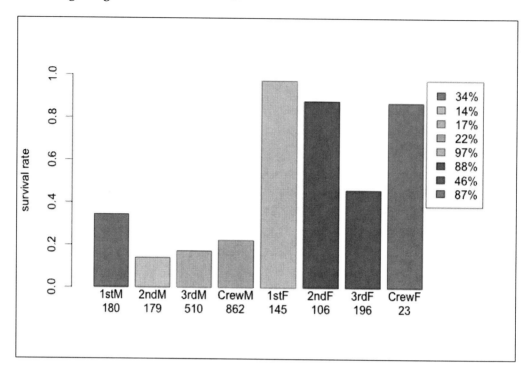

We can find the number of passengers of a group under its column. Apart from the female crew, each bar contains at least 100 passengers, so we can assume that the result is meaningful. In order to measure the meaningfulness, we could have used a statistic technique such as confidence intervals or a hypothesis test, but it's not the topic of this book.

The class is affecting the males and the females in different ways. In the case of males, the survival rate is very low although it is significantly higher for the first class. In the case of females, the survival rate is close to 100 percent for each class apart from the third class.

We can also look at the chart in the opposite way in order to understand the impact of the gender over the passengers belonging to the same class. In all the situations, the survival rate is significantly higher, although the difference is much higher for some specific classes. The impact of the gender and the class are related, so we need to take account of both the features at the same time if we want to understand their effect.

We haven't explored the age yet. We can visualize the survival rate for each combination of all the features. The code to prepare and plot the table is similar as before. In this case, we can just apply the operations to dtTitanic directly. The steps are as follows:

1. Compute the percentage of people that survived or didn't survive for each combination of the three features:

```
dtTitanic[, nTot := sum(Freq), by=c('Sex', 'Class', 'Age')]
```

2. Add the percentage of passengers surviving for each attribute combination:

```
dtTitanic[, percentage := Freq / nTot]
```

3. Extract the survival rate using the Survived == 'Yes' condition:

```
dtAll <- dtTitanic[Survived == 'Yes', ]
```

4. Add the legend text including the abbreviations of all the three features. For the class, we use substring that is a function extracting a part of the string. In our case, we extract the first character, so we specify that we extract the elements between 1 and 1 using substring(Class, 1, 1):

```
dtAll[, ClassAbbr := substring(Class, 1, 1)]
dtAll[, SexAbbr := ifelse(Sex == 'Male', 'M', 'F')]
dtAll[, AgeAbbr := ifelse(Age == 'Child', 'C', 'A')]
dtAll[, textLegend := paste(ClassAbbr, SexAbbr, AgeAbbr, sep='')];
```

5. Add the plot color:

```
dtAll[, colorPlot := rainbow(nrow(dtAll))]
```

6. Add the percentage to display in the label:

```
dtAll[, labelPerc := paste(round(percentage * 100), '%', sep='')]
```

7. Add the label including the percentage and the total number:

```
dtAll[, label := paste(labelPerc, nTot, sep='\n')]
```

8. Generate the plot. We have more groups than before, so the layout is different in order to visualize all the relevant information. The xlim argument leaves some space for the legend and the cex.names argument decreases the label text size:

```
barplot(
  height=dtAll[, percentage],
  names.arg=dtAll[, label],
  col=dtAll[, colorPlot],
  xlim=c(0, 23),
```

```
        legend.text=dtAll[, textLegend],
        cex.names=0.5
    )
```

The histogram is as follows:

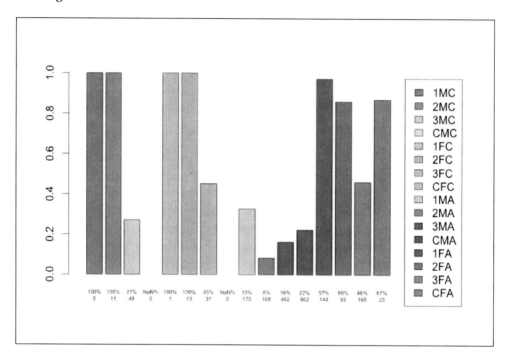

The legend displays the abbreviated feature combinations. For instance, **1MC** means first class, male, child. In the case of combinations with no passengers, we don't have any information about the percentage, so the bar label displays **NaN%**.

Since we are combining three features, some groups are very small. For instance, we have only five first class male children. There are also other groups with no passengers at all (for example, children in the crew). Therefore, this approach has some limitations.

# Exploring the data using machine learning models

Visualizing the survival rate for each group of passengers provides us with an overview of the data. We have an idea about how the different features interact with the survival rate and with each other. For instance, we know that the social class has a different impact on the survival rate depending on the gender. But which of the two features has the highest impact? How big is the impact of each feature? We haven't defined a ranking of the features or quantified the impact of each of them. Some machine learning techniques allow us to investigate further, answering to our questions.

# Exploring the data using a decision tree

We have three features (class, sex, and age) and we want to divide the passengers in groups accordingly. We can't define a group for each combination of features since we won't have enough data for some groups such as the female children of the first class. A solution is to divide the passengers in groups in such a way that each group contains enough data. A group is defined by some conditions on the features, such as males not belonging to the first class. The groups should cover every possible situation without overlapping. A machine learning technique that identifies groups that are big enough is the decision tree learning.

There is a new passenger and we know it's a male child of the second class. We don't know if the passenger will survive or not and we want to predict that. How can we use the data? We can check whether the passenger is a male or a female. Accordingly, with our previous data exploration, he'll survive with a probability of 21 percent since he's a male. Taking account of the social class, we can say that he will survive with a probability of 14 percent. There are 179 second class male passengers, so this result is meaningful. Then, knowing that he is a child, we can check the survival rate of the second class male children, which is 100 percent. Does it make sense to say that he will survive with a probability of 100 percent? There are only 11 passengers that are second class male children, so we don't have enough data to make an accurate prediction. Should we use the survival rate of the second class males? What if we use the survival rate of all the male children instead? What about the second class children? There are different options leading to different results.

A solution is to identify the key features and take account of them only. For instance, if the gender and class are the two most important features, we can use them to make a prediction. However, in the case of the third class male children, we have much more data than the first class male children. What if we take account of the age only in the case of third class males? The number of features that we want to include depends on the group we're taking account of.

Instead of just selecting the two most important features, we can define a criterion of splitting a group only if it is big enough and we can visualize this principle through a decision tree. Let's suppose that in the beginning all the passengers belong to the same group. We can split them in two groups based on gender. Then, we can split the males in two groups: first class on one side and all the other classes on the other side. For the females, the most meaningful split might be another: children on one side, the adults on the other.

The decision tree learning technique learns from the data in order to identify the most meaningful splits and it can be used to explore the data. The tree continues splitting the data until the groups, defined by the tree leaves, are too small. Then, for each group, we use the related data to define an attribute that can be:

- **Categoric**: This is an attribute whose value belongs to categories. In this case, the categories are **Survived** and **Not survived**. The tree performs classification.

- **Numeric**: This is an attribute that can be measured, and in this case it is the survival rate. The tree performs regression.

We can build a decision tree in R using the `rpart` package. In addition, we can visualize the trees using another package that is `rpart.plot`. In order to use the packages, we need to install and load them. In and case of installation issues, you can specify the repository as an argument of `install.packages`:

```
install.packages('rpart')
install.packages('rpart.plot')
```

After the installation, we can load both the packages:

```
library('rpart')
library('rpart.plot')
```

The starting point is `dtTitanic` and it contains a row for each combination of the features. Before building the decision tree, we need to transform the data into another format. We need to have a row for each passenger and the same columns apart from `Freq`. In order to generate the new table in the new format, we use the data table operation with `list` and `by`.

For each row of dtTitanic, we want to generate a table having a number of rows equal to Freq. Each row corresponds to a combination between Survived, Sex, Age, and Class, so the by argument contains a vector with the four features.

In the new table, each row contains a passenger, so Freq is equal to 1. Then, for each row of dtTitanic, we need to define a vector having Freq elements equal to 1. In order to do that, we use rep that is a function replicating an element a defined number of times. In our case, we use rep(1, Freq)). The other columns replicate the elements defined in by that are Survived, Sex, Age, and Class, so we don't need to redefine them:

```
dtLong <- dtTitanic[
  , list(Freq = rep(1, Freq)),
  by=c('Survived', 'Sex', 'Age', 'Class')
  ]
```

Freq is 1 for each row, so we don't need it anymore and can delete it:

```
dtLong[, Freq := NULL]
```

In order to build a decision tree showing the survival rate, we need to change the format of Survived. Instead of having No and Yes, we want 0 and 1 respectively. To modify the column, we can use ifelse:

```
dtLong[, Survived := ifelse(Survived == 'Yes', 1, 0)]
```

Let's see the first six rows of DtLong using head:

```
head(dtLong)
    Survived  Sex    Age Class
1:         0 Male Child   3rd
2:         0 Male Child   3rd
3:         0 Male Child   3rd
4:         0 Male Child   3rd
5:         0 Male Child   3rd
6:         0 Male Child   3rd
```

The first six rows show six male children that didn't survive.

The dtLong object contains the standard input of the decision tree algorithm and we can use rpart to build the model. Our goal is to define groups of passengers about whom we are able to estimate the survival rate:

```
help(rpart)
```

The mandatory arguments are:

- `formula`: This is a formula object defining the attribute to predict and the feature used to predict. The formula is defined by a string such as `outcome ~ feature1 + feature2 + feature3`.

- `data`: This is the data frame or data table that is `dtLong` in our case.

We need to define the formula starting from the `Survived ~ Sex + Age + Class` string:

```
formulaRpart <- formula('Survived ~ Sex + Age + Class')
```

Now we can build `treeRegr` containing a decision tree. Since `Survived` is numeric, the function automatically builds a `regrssion` tree:

```
treeRegr <- rpart(
  formula=formulaRpart,
  data=dtLong
)
```

The `treeRegr` object contains the decision tree and we can visualize it using `prp(treeRegr)`:

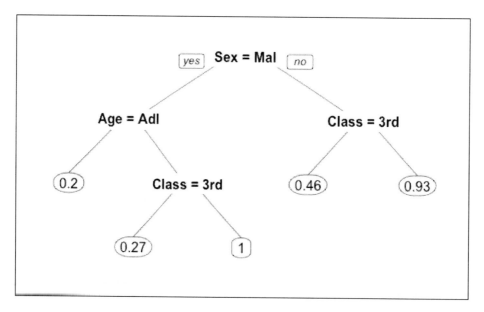

Let's take a look at the tree. Each interior node is labeled with a condition that splits the data in two parts. The node on the top, for instance, splits the passengers into males and females. The branch on the left corresponds to the passengers fulfilling the condition (in this case, the male passengers), and the branch on the right corresponds to the others (the females). Each leaf defines the survival rate of the group. For instance, the leaf to the right states that the survival rate for the females not belonging to the third class is 93 percent.

The tree doesn't contain all the possible feature combinations because of the lack of data. For instance, in the case of the females, there are only 45 children and they belong to different social classes, so the tree doesn't divide the females based on their age.

Let's suppose that we have a new passenger that is female, child, second class. How do we predict if she will survive? She is a female not belonging to the third class, so her expected survival rate is 93 percent. Therefore, we can say that she will likely survive.

The tree defines a survival rate that is a number. What if we wanted to predict whether the passenger survived or not? We can build a classification tree adding method='class' input to rpart:

```
treeClass = rpart(
    formula='Survived ~ Sex + Age + Class',
    data=dtLong,
    method='class'
)
prp(treeClass)
```

The tree is shown as follows:

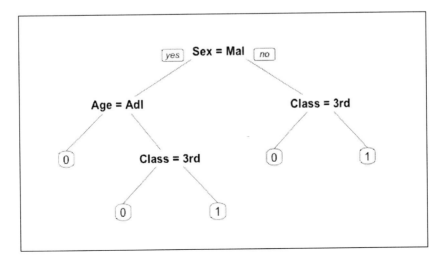

This tree predicts that the only passengers that will survive are females and children not belonging to the third class. This result is useful to explore the data. The next step is using machine learning models to predict an outcome. We can use this tree for that purpose, although it just defines five groups of passengers out of the 16 possible feature combinations, so it might not be the most appropriate technique. There are more advanced algorithms and in the next chapter we see one of them.

# Predicting newer outcomes

Given a new passenger and knowing his or her personal information, we want to predict whether he or she will survive. The options that we explored until now are based on dividing the passengers into groups and identifying the survival rate for each group. For some combinations of features, such as first class female children, we don't have enough data, so we have to use the survival rate of a larger group such as females not belonging to the third class. We are ignoring some details, for instance, the fact that they are children, and in this way we are losing information. Is there a way to estimate the survival rate for any combination of features, regardless of how many passengers we have?

There are many machine learning algorithms that take account of all the features at the same time. In this chapter, we see a very popular algorithm that is the **random forest** algorithm. It's not the best option in this context, as it performs better when there are much more features, but it's good for the purpose of illustrating a general approach.

# Building a machine learning model

As its name suggests, the random forest algorithm is based on many random decision trees. The algorithm builds `ntree` trees repeating the following steps:

1.  Generate the data to build the tree choosing a random row from the data (in our case, that is `dtLong`) sampsize times. Each row can be chosen more than once and in the end we have a table with sampsize random rows.

2.  Randomly select a `mtry` number of features (unfortunately in our case we don't have many features, but it's still possible to select a subset of them).

3.  Build a decision tree based on the sampled data taking account of the selected features only.

A random forest model is composed by `ntree` decision trees. In our context, given a new passenger, the model forecasts their survival rate using each tree. The final forecasted value is the average between the survival rates. In another variation of the algorithm, we have the mode instead of the average.

The random forest is a popular algorithm and it is provided by the `randomForest` package. Let's install and load it:

```
install.packages('randomForest')
library('randomForest')
```

Like the simple decision tree learning, the random forest attributes can be categoric or numeric.

In our case, all the features are categoric and there are two to four possible values for each feature. We can convert the features into a numeric format. For instance, in the case of `Sex`, the possible values are `Male` and `Female`. We can define a numeric feature that is `1` in the case of `Male` and `0` otherwise. The new feature shows the same information in a different way. Numeric features derived from categoric in this way are called dummy variables. In the case of a categoric feature with more than two categories, we can define a dummy variable for each categories apart from one. In this way, looking at the dummy variables, if one of them is equal to `1`, we know which the groups are. If they are all equal to `0`, we know that a group is remaining.

We can define a new table containing dummy variables through the following steps:

1.  Build a copy of the categoric features table:

    ```
    dtDummy <- copy(dtLong)
    ```

2.  Convert `Sex` into a dummy variable:

    ```
    dtDummy[, Male := Sex == 'Male']
    dtDummy[, Sex := NULL]
    ```

3.  Convert `Age` into a dummy variable:

    ```
    dtDummy[, Child := Age == 'Child']
    dtDummy[, Age := NULL]
    ```

4.  Convert `Class` into three dummy variables:

    ```
    dtDummy[, Class1 := Class == '1st']
    dtDummy[, Class2 := Class == '2nd']
    dtDummy[, Class3 := Class == '3rd']
    dtDummy[, Class := NULL]
    ```

5.  Define the `formulaRf` formula:

    ```
    formulaRf <- formula('Survived ~ Male + Child + Class1 + Class2 +
    Class3')
    ```

6. Build `forest` containing the random forest model. All the parameters are left as their default values:

```
forest <- randomForest(
  formula=formulaRf,
  data=dtDummy
)
```

We stored the random forest model in `forest` that is a list containing the machine learning model, and all the related parameters and information. We can explore the model observing the elements of the list. For instance, the number of trees that the model has built is contained in the `ntree` element:

```
forest$ntree
[1] 500
```

Another parameter is `mtry` and it defines the number of variables used in each iteration:

```
forest$mtry
[1] 1
```

The number of trees has been defaulted to 500.

The algorithm is selecting just one feature at once. The reason is that the random forest is meant to work with a lot of features, so it doesn't perform well in this context.

Another parameter is `type` and it defines the output of the algorithm. The random forest can be used for different purposes and in our case we want to estimate the survival rate, so we want to use it for regression:

```
forest$type
[1] "regression"
```

As expected, `forest` is performing regression.

If we want to change some parameters, we can define them in the arguments. In this chapter, we are not defining a criterion to set the parameters, so we just assign another value. For instance, we can build `1000` trees using three random features and `1500` random rows for each. We can rebuild `forest` changing the parameters:

```
forest <- randomForest(
  formula=formulaRf,
  data=dtDummy,
  ntree=1000,
```

```
    mtry=3,
    sampsize=1500
)
```

We built a random `forest` model and the next subsection shows how to use it.

# Using the model to predict new outcomes

Now that we have built the model, we can use it to perform some predictions. If we have a new passenger, what is their survival rate? First, let's extract a random passenger:

```
rowRandom <- dtDummy[100]
rowRandom
    Survived Freq Male Child Class1 Class2 Class3
1:        No    1 TRUE FALSE    TRUE  FALSE  FALSE
```

The random passenger is an adult male of the first class. We can use the `forest` model to estimate his survival rate. The `predict` function allows us to apply the model on the new data, obtaining a prediction:

```
predict(forest, rowRandom)
        1
0.3830159
```

The estimated survival rate is about 38 percent, so the passenger won't likely survive. We can use the same approach to predict the survival rate of all the passengers. However, that means to apply the model on the same data that we used to build it. This approach is not good for testing the model because the predicted values will be related to the initial data. Keeping in mind that this result cannot be used, we can use it just to compare the prediction with the real data:

```
prediction = predict(forest, dtDummy)
```

We can see the prediction of six random rows using `sample`:

```
sample(prediction, 6)
     1895       448       967      1553      1683         4
0.6934046 0.2260507 0.2499303 0.3830159 0.2260507 0.2974706
```

We defined a survival rate for each passenger. Let's add the estimated survival rate to the `dtDummy` table:

```
dtDummy[, SurvivalRatePred := predict(forest, dtDummy)]
```

Now, we can predict that a passenger will survive if their survival rate is above a threshold, for instance, 50 percent. We can define a new column name, `SurvivedPred`, containing our prediction:

```
dtDummy[, SurvivedPred := ifelse(SurvivalRatePred > 0.5, 1, 0)]
```

Now we can compare the predicted survival with the initial data. In order to evaluate how many times the two values match, we can define an `error` column that is `TRUE` if the values don't match:

```
dtDummy[, error := SurvivedPred != Survived]
```

Starting from the error column, we can compute the general error as the percentage of passengers upon which we made a wrong prediction. We need to divide the number of errors by the number of passengers. We can have the number of errors applying sum to error, since the sum of a vector of Boolean variables is equal to the number of `TRUE` values. The total number of passengers is defined by `.N`, which in the `data.table` notation is equal to the number of rows:

```
percError <- dtDummy[, sum(error) / .N]
percError
[1] 0.2094502
```

The model predicted the wrong outcome in 21 percent of the situations, so we have an accuracy of 79 percent. Anyway, this result doesn't make any sense since we're making a prediction on the same data that we used to build the model. In addition, knowing how many passengers survived, we could have just guessed the most common outcome for each of them. If more than half of them survived, we can set `SurvivedPred` = `TRUE` for all of them and guess more than half. Let's compute the overall probability of surviving. The general survival rate is lower than 50 percent, so each passenger is more likely not to survive. Then, in absence of any other information, we can predict that no one survives:

```
dtTitanic[Survived == 'No', sum(Freq)] / dtTitanic[, sum(Freq)]
[1] 0.676965
```

We could have achieved accuracy of more than 65 percent without taking account of any feature, so 79 percent is just 15 percent higher. In addition, as already said, this accuracy cannot be used because we are applying the model on the same data used to build it.

# Validating a model

In order to evaluate the real accuracy of a model, we can build it using a part of the data, such as 80 percent of the passengers. Then, we can apply the model on the remaining 20 percent of data. The data that we use to build the model is called the **training set** and the other is called the **test set**.

We can assign each row to the training set with a probability of 80 percent. In this way, the training set will include about 80 percent of the data. In order to define which rows should be included in the training set, we can define a logical vector, called `indexTrain`, which is TRUE for each row belonging to the training set. We can generate the vector using sample and the arguments are:

- `x`: This represents the possible values; in this case, TRUE and FALSE
- `size`: This represents the vector length; in this case, it is equal to the number of rows in dtDummy
- `replace`: If the value is TRUE, each value (TRUE or FALSE) can be sampled more than once
- `prob`: This is a vector with the probabilities of sampling the values of x; in this case, it is `c(0.8, 0.2)`

Consider the following code:

```
indexTrain <- sample(
  x=c(TRUE, FALSE),
  size=nrow(dtDummy),
  replace=TRUE,
  prob=c(0.8, 0.2)
)
```

Now, we can extract the rows in which `indexTrain` is equal to TRUE:

```
dtTrain <- dtDummy[indexTrain]
```

In the same way, we extract the rows of the test set. The `!` operator means NOT and it allows the rows for which `indexTrain` is equal to FALSE to be extracted:

```
dtTest <- dtDummy[!indexTrain]
```

Now, we can build the model using the same parameters as before. Knowing that we have less data, we can just reduce the sampsize parameters that define the data to use for each tree:

```
forest <- randomForest(
   formula=formulaRf,
   data=dtTrain,
   ntree=1000,
   mtry=3,
   sampsize=1200
)
```

We built a model without taking account of dtTest, so we can use it to predict on dtTest. Like before, we predict that a passenger will survive if their survival rate is above 50 percent. After the prediction, we can estimate the error, using the same R commands as before:

```
dtTest[, SurvivalRatePred := predict(forest, dtTest)]
dtTest[, SurvivedPred := ifelse(SurvivalRatePred > 0.5, 1, 0)]
dtTest[, error := SurvivedPred != Survived]
percError <- dtTest[, sum(error) / .N]
percError
[1] 0.2416107
```

The estimated error, percError, depends on how we have split the data, so it's different every time we define a new random training/test split. However, we can repeat the steps many times and compute the average error. This approach is called cross validation and it's a very useful tool to estimate the accuracy.

This chapter showed a generic approach to build and validate a machine learning model. Using this approach, we can forecast an attribute and estimate the prediction accuracy.

# Summary

In this chapter, we learned how to process data using data table operations and built some simple R plots for exploratory data analysis. We learned how to use decision trees to find useful insights and build machine learning models (random forest) to perform predictions. We saw how to change the parameters of a model and how to validate it.

The next three chapters show the steps introduced in this chapter in detail.
*Chapter 4, Step 1 - Data Exploration and Feature Engineering,* shows the first step of machine learning that consists of data exploration and feature engineering, in depth.

# 4
# Step 1 – Data Exploration and Feature Engineering

There are different kinds of problems that require a machine learning solution. For instance, our target can be forecasting future outcomes or identifying patterns from the data. The starting point is a set of objects (for example, items) or people (for example, customers of a supermarket). In most situations, a machine learning technique identifies the solution, starting from some features that describe objects/ people. The features are numeric and/or categorical attributes, and they are the base of the machine learning model. Having the right features will improve the performance and accuracy of the model, so it is extremely important to define some features that are relevant to the problem.

In this chapter, you will:

- Build machine learning solutions
- Build a feature data
- Clean the data
- Explore the defined features
- Modify the features
- Rank the features using a filter

# Building a machine learning solution

In which stage of a machine learning solution are we defining the features? Let's look at an overview of the whole procedure of building the solution. We can divide the approach into three steps:

1. Define the features that we will be using.
2. Apply one or more techniques to solve the problem.
3. Evaluate the result and optimize the performance.

In the first step, we can evaluate the relevance of each feature by using a filter and selecting the most relevant feature. We can also define a combination of some features that are good for describing the data.

In the second step, when we build a model, we can use some techniques (embedded methods) that rank the features and identify the most relevant feature automatically.

The last step is very important since we have more information, allowing us to identify a more proper feature set. For instance, we can use the same model with different sets of features and evaluate which feature combination performs better. An option is to use a wrapper that consists of building a model with a chosen set of features, iteratively add (or remove) a feature, and retain the change if it improves the accuracy of the model.

In conclusion, a feature selection is a cycle rather than a step, and it takes place in each part of the procedure. This chapter shows the feature engineering process, which consists of defining the features, transforming them, and identifying their ranking. The steps are:

- Exploring the data
- Defining/transforming new features
- Identifying the most relevant features

Although exploring the data is always at the beginning, all the steps can be repeated until we find a satisfying solution, so they don't always follow the same order. For instance, after identifying the most relevant features, we can explore the data, identify new patterns, and consequently define some new features.

The process of feature selection is related to the model, and in this chapter, we identify some features that are suitable for many models.

This chapter shows an example of flags. Based on the flag of a country, our target is to determine the country's language. Assuming that we know the flags of all the countries and the language of only some of them, the model will estimate the language of the others.

# Building the feature data

This section shows how we can structure the raw data to build the features. For each country, the data is:

- A picture of the flag
- Some geographical data such as continent, geographic quadrant, area, and population
- The language and religion of the country

The target is to build a model that predicts a country language starting from its flag. Most of the models can deal with numeric and/or categorical data, so we can't use the image of the flag as a feature for the model. The solution is to define some features, for instance the number of colors, that describe each flag. In this way, we start from a table whose rows correspond to the countries and whose columns correspond to the flag features.

It would take a lot of time to build the matrix with the flag attributes based on the pictures. Fortunately, we can use a dataset that contains some features. The data that we have is still a bit messy, so we need to clean and transform it to build a feature table in the *right format*.

The features contained in the dataset display some information about:

- The colors in the flag
- The patterns in the flag
- Some additional elements in the flag, such as text or some stars
- Some geographical data, such as continent, geographic quadrant, area, and population
- The language and religion of the country

The steps to lead the table in the right format are as follows:

1. Download the dataset and the related information from `https://archive.ics.uci.edu/ml/machine-learning-databases/flags/` and download `flag.data`.

2. Open RStudio and set the working directory to the folder that contains the data:

```
setwd('path/containing/the/data')
```

3. Load the data into the R environment:

```
dfFlag <- read.csv('flag.data', header=FALSE)
```

Now, we can see the structure of `dfFlag` using `str`:

```
str(dfFlag)
'data.frame':    194 obs. of  30 variables:
 $ V1 : Factor w/ 194 levels "Afghanistan",..:
  1 2 3 4 5 6 7 8 9 10 ...
 $ V2 : int  5 3 4 6 3 4 1 1 2 2 ...
 $ V3 : int  1 1 1 3 1 2 4 4 3 3 ...
 $ V4 : int  648 29 2388 0 0 1247 0 0 2777 2777 ...
 $ V5 : int  16 3 20 0 0 7 0 0 28 28 ...
 $ V6 : int  10 6 8 1 6 10 1 1 2 2 ...
 $ V7 : int  2 6 2 1 0 5 1 1 0 0 ...
 $ V8 : int  0 0 2 0 3 0 0 0 0 0 ...
 $ V9 : int  3 0 0 0 0 2 1 1 3 3 ...
 $ V10: int  5 3 3 5 3 3 3 5 2 3 ...
 $ V11: int  1 1 1 1 1 1 0 1 0 0 ...
 $ V12: int  1 0 1 0 0 0 0 0 0 0 ...
 $ V13: int  0 0 0 1 1 0 1 1 1 1 ...
 $ V14: int  1 1 0 1 1 1 0 1 0 1 ...
 $ V15: int  1 0 1 1 0 0 1 1 1 1 ...
 $ V16: int  1 1 0 0 0 1 0 1 0 0 ...
 $ V17: int  0 0 0 1 0 0 1 0 0 0 ...
 $ V18: Factor w/ 8 levels "black","blue",..:
  5 7 5 2 4 7 8 7 2 2 ...
 $ V19: int  0 0 0 0 0 0 0 0 0 0 ...
 $ V20: int  0 0 0 0 0 0 0 0 0 0 ...
 $ V21: int  0 0 0 0 0 0 0 0 0 0 ...
 $ V22: int  0 0 0 0 0 0 0 0 0 0 ...
 $ V23: int  1 1 1 0 0 1 0 1 0 1 ...
 $ V24: int  0 0 1 0 0 0 0 0 0 0 ...
 $ V25: int  0 0 0 1 0 0 0 1 0 0 ...
 $ V26: int  1 0 0 1 0 1 0 0 0 0 ...
```

```
$ V27: int   0 1 0 1 0 0 1 0 0 0 ...
$ V28: int   0 0 0 0 0 0 0 0 0 0 ...
$ V29: Factor w/ 7 levels "black","blue",..:
  1 6 4 2 2 6 7 1 2 2 ...
$ V30: Factor w/ 8 levels "black","blue",..:
  5 7 8 7 7 1 2 7 2 2 ...
```

The df Flag object contains 30 columns whose names are not defined. We have documentation that describes the data contained in flag.description.txt, which allows us to define the column names. The first seven columns contain some attributes that are not related to the flag. Let's start defining some vectors that contain the feature names. The first column is the name of the country. These are the steps to define the names:

1.  Define the country name:

    ```
    nameCountry <- 'name'
    ```

2.  Define the names of three geographic features: continent, zone, and area:

    ```
    namesGeography <- c('continent', 'zone', 'area')
    ```

3.  Define the names of three features of the countries' citizens, including their language:

    ```
    namesDemography <- c('population', 'language',
      'religion')
    ```

4.  Define a unique vector that contains the seven attributes in the right order:

    ```
    namesAttributes <- c(nameCountry, namesGeography,
      namesDemography)
    ```

5.  Define the names of the features defining the number of bars, stripes, and colors:

    ```
    namesNumbers <- c('bars', 'stripes', 'colors')
    ```

6.  For some colors, there is a variable that displays 1 if the flag contains the color and 0 otherwise. Define their names:

    ```
    namesColors <- c('red', 'green', 'blue', 'gold', 'white', 'black',
      'orange')
    ```

7.  Define the name of the predominant color:

    ```
    nameMainColor <- 'mainhue'
    ```

8. Define the name of the attributes that display how many patterns/drawings (for instance, a shape, a picture, or a text) are contained in the flag:

```
namesDrawings <- c(
  'circles', 'crosses', 'saltires', 'quarters',
  'sunstars', 'crescent', 'triangle', 'icon',
    'animate', 'text'
)
```

9. Dangles: the color in two out of the four angles:

```
namesAngles <- c('topleft', 'botright')
```

10. Define `namesFlag` that contains all the names in the right order:

```
namesFlag <- c(namesNumbers, namesColors, nameMainColor,
  namesDrawings, namesAngles)
```

11. Set the `dfFlag` column names that bind `namesAttributes` and `namesFlag`:

```
names(dfFlag) <- c(namesAttributes, namesFlag)
```

Now, the data frame has the right column names. However, some columns, such as `language` contain numbers instead of the attribute name, and the documentation shows what the numbers stand for. For instance, for language, 1 corresponds to English and 2 to Spanish. We can build a data table that has the data in the right format using the following steps:

1. Convert `dfFlag` into the `dtFlag` data table:

```
library(data.table)
dtFlag <- data.table(dfFlag)
```

2. Display the `continent` column:

```
dtFlag[1:20, continent]
[1]  5 3 4 6 3 4 1 1 2 2 6 3 1 5 5 1 3 1 4 1
```

3. The `continent` column contains a number between 1 and 6 and the documentation shows 1=N.America, 2=S.America, 3=Europe, 4=Africa, 5=Asia, 6=Oceania. Then, we define a vector that contains the continents:

```
vectorContinents <- c('N.America', 'S.America',
  'Europe', 'Africa', 'Asia', 'Oceania')
```

4.  Convert `continent` into `factor` whose levels are `vectorContinents`:

    ```
    dtFlag[, continent := factor(continent,
      labels=vectorContinents)]
    ```

5.  Similar to `continent`, convert `zone` into `factor`:

    ```
    vectorZones <- c('NE', 'SE', 'SW', 'NW')
    dtFlag[, zone := factor(zone, labels=vectorZones)]
    ```

6.  Convert `language` into `factor`:

    ```
    vectorLanguages <- c(
      'English', 'Spanish', 'French', 'German',
      'Slavic',
      'Other Indo-European', 'Chinese', 'Arabic',
      'Japanese/Turkish/Finnish/Magyar', 'Others')
      dtFlag[, language := factor(language,
      labels=vectorLanguages)]
    ```

7.  Convert `religion` into `factor`:

    ```
    vectorReligions <- c(
      'Catholic', 'Other Christian', 'Muslim',
      'Buddhist',
      'Hindu', 'Ethnic', 'Marxist', 'Others'
    )
    dtFlag[, religion := factor(religion,
      labels=vectorReligions)]
    ```

Let's take a look at `dtFlag`:

```
str(dtFlag)
Classes 'data.table' and 'data.frame':      194 obs. of  30
  variables:
 $ name      : Factor w/ 194 levels "Afghanistan",..: 1 2 3 4 5
  6 7 8 9 10 ...
 $ continent : int  5 3 4 6 3 4 1 1 2 2 ...
 $ zone      : Factor w/ 4 levels "NE","SE","SW",..: 1 1 1 3
  1 2 4 4 3 3 ...
 $ area      : int  648 29 2388 0 0 1247 0 0 2777 2777 ...
 $ population: int  16 3 20 0 0 7 0 0 28 28 ...
 $ language  : int  10 6 8 1 6 10 1 1 2 2 ...
 $ religion  : int  2 6 2 1 0 5 1 1 0 0 ...
 $ bars      : int  0 0 2 0 3 0 0 0 0 0 ...
 $ stripes   : int  3 0 0 0 0 2 1 1 3 3 ...
 $ colors    : int  5 3 3 5 3 3 3 5 2 3 ...
```

```
$ red       : int  1 1 1 1 1 0 1 0 0 ...
$ green     : int  1 0 1 0 0 0 0 0 0 ...
$ blue      : int  0 0 0 1 1 0 1 1 1 ...
$ gold      : int  1 1 0 1 1 1 0 1 0 1 ...
$ white     : int  1 0 1 1 0 0 1 1 1 ...
$ black     : int  1 1 0 0 0 1 0 1 0 0 ...
$ orange    : int  0 0 0 1 0 0 1 0 0 0 ...
$ mainhue   : Factor w/ 8 levels "black","blue",..: 5 7 5 2 4
  7 8 7 2 2 ...
$ circles   : int  0 0 0 0 0 0 0 0 0 0 ...
$ crosses   : int  0 0 0 0 0 0 0 0 0 0 ...
$ saltires  : int  0 0 0 0 0 0 0 0 0 0 ...
$ quarters  : int  0 0 0 0 0 0 0 0 0 0 ...
$ sunstars  : int  1 1 1 0 0 1 0 1 0 1 ...
$ crescent  : int  0 0 1 0 0 0 0 0 0 0 ...
$ triangle  : int  0 0 0 1 0 0 0 1 0 0 ...
$ icon      : int  1 0 0 1 0 1 0 0 0 0 ...
$ animate   : int  0 1 0 1 0 0 1 0 0 0 ...
$ text      : int  0 0 0 0 0 0 0 0 0 0 ...
$ topleft   : Factor w/ 7 levels "black","blue",..: 1 6 4 2 2
  6 7 1 2 2 ...
$ botright  : Factor w/ 8 levels "black","blue",..: 5 7 8 7 7
  1 2 7 2 2 ...
- attr(*, ".internal.selfref")=<externalptr>
```

The data is in the right format. Although we had to transform the data properly, it still took much less time than defining the features manually.

# Exploring and visualizing the features

After having defined the features, we can explore them and identify how they are related to the problem. In this section, you will see how to explore the data and define some simple charts.

Let's start with a feature, for instance, `mainhue`, which displays the predominant color of a flag. We want to identify the most common predominant colors, and for that purpose, we can use `table` to count the number of occurrences of each possible value. We can extract the `mainhue` column from `dtFlag` and apply `table` to it:

```
table(dtFlag[, mainhue])
 black   blue  brown   gold  green orange    red  white
     5     40      2     19     31      4     71     22
```

The three most common predominant colors are red, blue, and green. Please note that we could have put `table` inside the square brackets, obtaining the same result with cleaner code: `dtFlag[, table(mainhue)]`.

How can we perform the same operation over any other column? First, let's define a string called `nameCol` that contains the name of the column that we want to analyze. In order to access the column, we can use `get(nameCol)` inside the square brackets of `dtFlag`:

```
nameCol <- 'mainhue'
dtFlag[, table(get(nameCol))]
```

This notation is very useful because we can easily include it inside a function using the name string, visualizing the same results for all the other columns:

```
listTableCol = lapply(
   namesAngles, function(nameCol){
     dtFlag[, table(get(nameCol))]
   })
listTableCol[[1]]
   black    blue    gold   green orange      red   white
      12      43       6      32      4       56      41
```

What if we want to build a chart instead? We can build a histogram using `barplot`. Let's first extract the table with each value of frequency:

```
nameCol <- 'language'
freqValues <- dtFlag[, table(get(nameCol))]
```

The `freqValues` method contains the number of countries that speak any language in the list. We can extract a language vector using `names`:

```
names(freqValues)
```

Now, we have all the necessary data to build a histogram (see the documentation of `barplot` if you haven't read *Chapter 3, A Simple Machine Learning Analysis*). In addition, we can define the colors using `rainbow`:

```
barplot(
  height = freqValues,
  names.arg = names(freqValues),
  main = nameCol,
  col = rainbow(length(freqValues)),
  ylab = 'number of flags'
)
```

The histogram obtained is as follows:

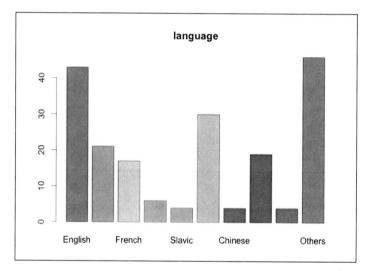

This chart is very useful if we want to explore an attribute. In order to do this using just one line of code, we can define a function that builds this chart for a generic column, `nameCol`. In addition, we can add `legend` that displays the percentage. In order to display `legend`, we compute `percValues`, which contains the percentage of rows that display that value, and use it as the `legend.text` argument, as shown:

```
barplotAttribute <- function(dtData, nameCol)
{
  # define the frequency
  freqValues <- dtData[, table(get(nameCol))]
  # define the percentage
  percValues <- freqValues / sum(freqValues)
  percValues <- round(percValues * 100)
  percValues <- paste(percValues, '%')
  # generate the histogram
  barplot(
```

```
    height = freqValues,
    names.arg = names(freqValues),
    main = nameCol,
    col = rainbow(length(freqValues)),
    legend.text = percValues,
    ylab = 'number of flags'
  )
}
```

Let's apply the function to another column, for instance `stripes`:

```
barplotAttribute(dtFlag, 'stripes')
```

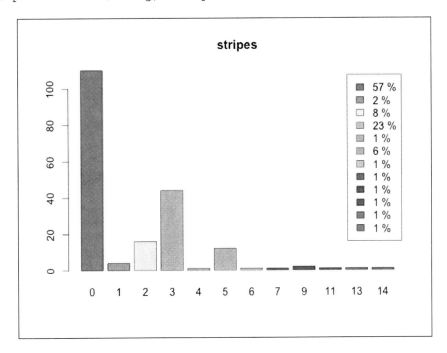

Using a `for` loop, we can generate the same chart for each flag attribute. We need time to see the result between, each chart and the following, so we stop the program using `readline`. The script pauses until we press *Enter* in the console. In this way, we can explore all the features very quickly, shown as follows:

```
for(nameCol in namesFlag)
{
  barplotAttribute(dtFlag, nameCol)
  readline()
}
```

With these few lines of code, we have observed how frequent the values of each feature are.

Another quick exploration is, given a color, counting the number of flags that contain the color. For instance, let's count the flags that have a red part. There is an attribute called `red` whose value is 1 if the flag contains a red part and 0 otherwise. If we sum up all the column values, we will obtain the total number of flags that contain a red part, as shown:

```
dtFlag[, sum(red)]
[1] 153
dtFlag[, sum(get('red'))]
[1] 153
```

As we have seen earlier, we can use `get` inside the square brackets. How can we do the same for all the common colors? The `namesColors` vector contains the name of all the color attributes, as shown:

```
namesColors
[1] "red"     "green"  "blue"    "gold"    "white"
   "black"   "orange"
```

The first element of `namesColors` is `red`, so we can use it to count the flags that contain red:

```
dtFlag[, sum(get(namesColors[1]))]
[1] 153
```

We can use `sapply` (see the documentation) to apply a function over each element of `namesColors`. In this case, the function counts the number of flags that contain a specific color:

```
sapply(namesColors, function(nameColor){
  dtFlag[, sum(get(nameColor))]
})
 red  green  blue  gold  white  black  orange
 153     91    99    91    146     52      26
```

The most common colors are red and green.

Until now, we have explored the flag's features; the next step is to see how they are related to the country's language. A fast way is to use a decision tree (see *Chapter 3, A Simple Machine Learning Analysis*).

First, let's import the packages to generate and visualize the decision tree:

```
library('rpart')
library('rpart.plot')
```

The decision tree model requires a formula object that defines the relationship between the variables. In this case, the formula is *language ~ feature1 + feature2 + ....* We can build the formula by adding all the names contained in `namesFlag` using a `for` loop, as shown:

```
formulaRpart <- 'language ~ '
for(name in namesFlag){
  formulaRpart <- paste(formulaRpart, '+', name)
}
formulaRpart <- formula(formulaRpart)
```

We can build the model using `rpart` and visualize the tree using `prp`:

```
tree <- rpart(formula=formulaRpart, data=dtFlag)
prp(tree)
```

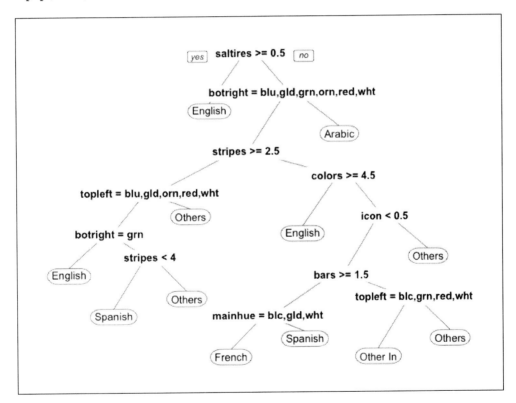

Some nodes of the tree are not clear to read. For instance, `saltires` displays 1 if the flag has a saltire, and 0 otherwise. The first tree node expresses the **saltires >= 0.5** condition, so the flags on the left have a saltire. This reflects the fact that the features are not in the appropriate format, so the next step will be to transform the feature.

First, let's define a new data table called `dtFeatures`, which contains the features and the outcome. From now, we will modify `dtFeatures` until all the features are in the right format, as shown:

```
dtFeatures <- dtFlag[, c('language', namesFlag), with=FALSE]
```

Let's define a function to visualize the table. We will reuse this function to keep track of progress during the feature transformation, as shown:

```
plotTree <- function(dtFeatures){
  formulaRpart <- paste(names(dtFeatures)[1], '~')
  for(name in names(dtFeatures)[-1]){
    formulaRpart <- paste(formulaRpart, '+', name)
  }
  formulaRpart <- formula(formulaRpart)
  tree <- rpart(formula=formulaRpart, data=dtFeatures)
  prp(tree)
}
plotTree(dtFeatures)
```

The chart is exactly the same as before.

So far, we have seen some techniques to explore the features. The data exploration allowed us to investigate the data nature, and it's the starting point to clean the current features and define some others. In addition, we have built some functions that allow us to generate some charts using just one line of code. We can use these functions to keep track of the feature transformation.

# Modifying the features

Our features are attributes that describe the flag, and some of them might not be in the right format. In this section, we will take a look at each feature and transform it if necessary.

In order to keep track of which features we have already processed, let's start defining an empty vector `namesProcessed`, which contains the features that we have already processed. When we transform a feature, we add the feature name into `namesProcessed`:

```
namesProcessed <- c()
```

Let's start with the numeric columns, such as `red`, which have two possible outcomes: 0, in case the flag contains red and 1 otherwise. The `red` variable defines an attribute, so it should be categorical instead of numeric. Then, we can convert `red` into a feature that is `yes` if the color is red and `no` otherwise.

If we take a look at the charts of each feature, we notice that some of them display only two values that are always `0` and `1`. In order to convert each of them into the `yes` and `no` format, we can use a `for` loop. For each feature in `namesFlag`, we check if there are only two possible values. If so, we convert the feature into a factor. Let's start with `red`:

```
nameFeat <- 'red'
```

We can check if `nameFeat` displays two values:

```
length(unique(dtFeatures[, get(nameFeat)])) == 2
```

In this case, the answer is `TRUE`, so we can generate a vector that contains the same column with `no` and `yes` for `0` and `1` respectively. For this purpose, we use `factor`, which specifies that the labels are `no` and `yes`, as shown:

```
vectorFactor <- dtFeatures[
   , factor(get(nameFeat), labels=c('no', 'yes'))
]
head(vectorFactor)
[1] yes yes yes yes yes yes
Levels: no yes
```

Now, we can convert each feature that displays two possible outcomes using a `for` loop. For each feature, we check whether it has only two values using `if`. After we generate `vectorFactor`, we override the old column using `eval` inside the square brackets. Doing `dtFeatures[, eval('red') := vectorFactor]` is the same as `dtFeatures[, red := vectorFactor]`, shown as follows:

```
for(nameFeat in namesFlag){
  if(length(unique(dtFeatures[, get(nameFeat)])) == 2){
    vectorFactor <- dtFeatures[
       , factor(get(nameFeat), labels=c('no', 'yes'))]
    dtFeatures[, eval(nameFeat) := vectorFactor]
    namesProcessed <- c(namesProcessed, nameFeat)
  }
}
```

Let's take a look at the features that we haven't transformed yet. The `namesFlag` feature contains all the initial features, and `namesProcessed` contains the ones that we have already transformed. In order to visualize the features that are not in `namesProcessed`, we can use `setdiff`, which is a function that gives the elements that are in the first vector and not in the second, as shown:

```
setdiff(namesFlag, namesProcessed)
```

There are still many features that we haven't analyzed yet. For instance, `bars` is a numeric attribute that displays the number of vertical bars in a flag. If we use `bars` as a numeric feature, the model will identify a relationship between the language and the model. All flags of the Spanish-speaking countries contain zero or three bars, so model can learn something like "the language can be Spanish only if we have less than four bars." However, there is no Spanish-speaking country whose flag has 1 or 2 bars. A solution is to group the countries on the basis of the number of bars, as shown:

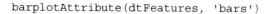

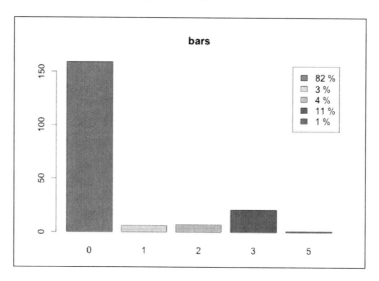

The chart shows that the groups with a significant number of flags are the **0** and **3** bars. Therefore, the groups can be as follows:

- Flags with no bars
- Flags with three bars
- All the other flags

We can define a new column named `nBars0`, which is equal to TRUE if the flag has no vertical bars:

```
dtFeatures[, nBars0 := bars == 0]
```

Similarly, we define `nBars3`, which is TRUE for the flags with three bars. We don't need to define a column with the remaining flags because they can already be identified by checking that `nBars0` and `nBars3` are FALSE:

```
dtFeatures[, nBars1_2 := bars %in% c(1, 2)]
dtFeatures[, nBars3 := bars == 3]
```

Let's remove the initial `bars` column and add `bars` to `namesProcessed`:

```
dtFeatures[, bars := NULL]
namesProcessed <- c(namesProcessed, 'bars')
```

The operation that we performed is called **discretization** because we generated some discrete features, starting from a numeric one.

Similarly, we can transform `stripes` and `colors`:

```
barplotAttribute(dtFeatures, 'stripes')
dtFeatures[, nStrp0 := stripes == 0]
dtFeatures[, nStrp2 := stripes == 2]
dtFeatures[, nStrp3 := stripes == 3]
dtFeatures[, nStrp5 := stripes == 5]
dtFeatures[, stripes := NULL]
namesProcessed <- c(namesProcessed, 'stripes')

barplotAttribute(dtFeatures, 'colors')
dtFeatures[, nCol12 := colors %in% c(1, 2)]
dtFeatures[, nCol3 := colors == 3]
dtFeatures[, nCol4_5 := colors %in% c(4, 5)]
dtFeatures[, colors := NULL]
namesProcessed <- c(namesProcessed, 'colors')
```

Let's take a look at the features contained in `namesDrawings` that we haven't processed yet:

```
for(nameCol in setdiff(namesDrawings, namesProcessed)){
  barplotAttribute(dtFeatures, nameCol)
  readline()
}
```

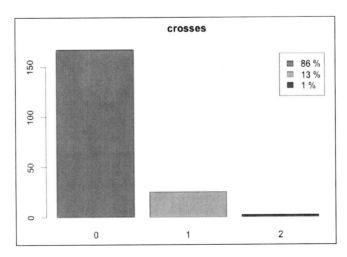

In all these features, most of the flags display 0. Therefore, we can group the flags into two categories: 0 and the rest. We are defining a new categorical variable that is yes if the value is greater than 0 and no otherwise. The process is called **binarization** because we transform some numeric features into categorical features that display two values only, as shown:

```
for(nameCol in setdiff(namesDrawings, namesProcessed)){
  dtFeatures[, eval(nameCol) := ifelse(get(nameCol) > 0, 'yes',
    'no')]
  namesProcessed <- c(namesProcessed, nameCol)
}
```

Let's explore the remaining features, as shown in the following code:

```
for(nameCol in setdiff(namesFlag, namesProcessed)){
  barplotAttribute(dtFeatures, nameCol)
  readline()
}
```

The chart obtained is as follows:

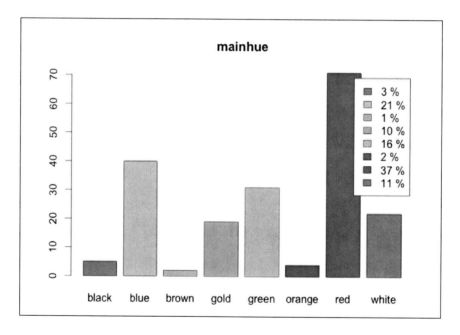

The three remaining features are `topleft`, `botright`, and `mainhue`. They are all categorical and display more than two possible values. For instance, there are eight options for `mainhue`. However, only a few flags have `black`, `brown`, or `orange` as their main color. We don't have enough information to take into account the less common colors. In this case, we can define a new categorical variable called `dummy variable` for each of them. We can decide to define a dummy variable for each possible color with at least 15 flags. The situation is similar for `topleft` and `botright`, so we can transform all of them in the same way, as shown:

```
namesToDummy <- c("topleft", "botright", "mainhue")
for(nameCol in namesToDummy){
  frequencyColors <- dtFeatures[, list(.N), by=nameCol]
  for(color in frequencyColors[N > 20, get(nameCol)]){
    nameFeatNew <- paste(nameCol, color, sep='')
    dtFeatures[, eval(nameFeatNew) := get(nameCol) == color]
  }
  dtFeatures[, eval(nameCol) := NULL]
  namesProcessed <- c(namesProcessed, nameCol)
}
```

Now, we have transformed all the features. However, some of the new columns that we have defined are of the `logical` class. It's better to visualize them as categorical attributes that display `yes` or `no`, so it's best to transform them, as shown:

```
for(nameCol in names(dtFeatures)){
  if(dtFeatures[, class(get(nameCol))] == 'logical'){
    print(nameCol)
    dtFeatures[, eval(nameCol) := ifelse(get(nameCol), 'yes', 'no')]
  }
}
```

Let's see how the decision tree has changed using the following code:

```
plotTree(dtFeatures)
```

The chart obtained is as follows:

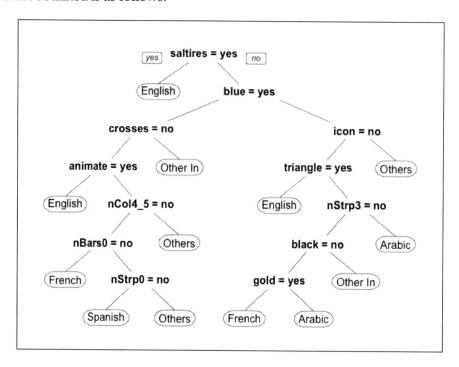

The decision tree is similar to the earlier tree. However, each node of the decision tree is checking a condition whose outcomes are yes and no.

In this chapter, we have seen three ways of transforming the features:

- **Discretization**: Starting from a numeric variable, we group all the possible values in sets. Then, for each set, we define a new variable that displays yes if the numeric variable belongs to the set and no otherwise.

- **Binarization**: Starting from a numeric variable, we discretize a numeric variable by defining two sets only. We define a threshold and we check whether the variable is above or below the threshold.

- **Dummy**: Starting from a categorical variable, we identify the most common outcomes. Then, for each common outcome, we define a new variable that displays yes if the variable is equal to the value and no otherwise.

# Ranking the features using a filter or a dimensionality reduction

In the previous section, we defined different features. But are all of them really relevant to the problem? There are some techniques called **embedded models** that automatically select the most relevant features. We can also build the same machine learning model using different sets of features and pick the set whose performance is better. Both the options are good, although they require a lot of computational power.

An alternative is to use filters that are techniques that identify the most relevant features. We use filters before applying any machine learning model, and in this way, we cut a lot of the computational cost of the algorithms. Some filters take account of each feature separately and are very computationally efficient.

A simple filter is the **Pearson correlation coefficient**, which is a measure of the linear relationship between variables. The correlation is a number between -1 and 1, and these two extreme values express a clear linear relationship between the two variables. When drawing a chart, all the points lie on the same line. A correlation of 0 expresses that there is no linear dependence between the two variables. The higher the correlation module, the stronger the linear relationship. In our case, we can measure the correlation between each flag attribute and the language, and pick the attributes whose correlation module is higher.

Another technique that takes account of each feature separately is the information-gain ratio. Let's suppose that we want to build a model without knowing anything about the flags. In this case, the best we can do is to identify the most common language and assume that each country speaks that language. What if we know only which flags contain the color red? The model will definitely be better than not having any information. How much better? The information-gain ratio of a feature is an index that quantifies the improvement that comes from adding the feature.

The correlation and information-gain ratio take account of each feature separately, so they completely ignore the interaction between them. For instance, we can have two features that have a high impact on the language and are so strongly related with each other that they contain the same information. Let's suppose that we have already included one of the two features in the model. Adding the other won't provide any further information, although it would be highly relevant by itself. If the relationship between the two features is linear, we talk about **multicollinearity**.

In other situations, we have two features that have a little relevance if taken separately and have a big impact if taken together. If we rank the features using this kind of filter, we will exclude both of them, losing some useful information.

An alternative to ranking the features is identifying relevant feature combinations. A technique is the **Principal component analysis (PCA)**, and it is based on the correlation between features. Starting from the features, the PCA defines a set of variables called principal components, which are linearly independent of each other. The number of principal components is equal to or less than the number of features and the components are ranked by variance. Then, it's possible to select a subset of components that have high variances. However, PCA has limitations since it is based on linear relationships only, and it doesn't take account of the attribute to predict things (language, in our example).

There are different techniques, and the one that we use in this chapter is the **information gain ratio** as it is simple and meaningful. R provides us with the FSelector package that contains different tools for the feature selection. The package requires you to have JRE installed on your computer, as shown:

```
install.packages('FSelector')
library('FSelector')
```

Let's build the namesFeatures vector that contains the name of all the features. Then, we can compute their information gain ratio using the information.gain function, as shown:

```
namesFeatures <- names(dtFeatures)[-1]
dfGains <- information.gain(language~., dtFeatures)
```

The dfGains method is a data frame with a field named attr_importance. The feature names are the row names, so let's add another column that contains the names:

```
dfGains$feature <- row.names(dfGains)
```

Let's convert the data frame into a data table:

```
dtGains <- data.table(dfGains)
```

In order to see the most relevant features, we can sort them by relevance:

```
dtGains <- dtGains[order(attr_importance, decreasing = T)]
  head(dtGains)
    attr_importance       feature
1:        0.1583055          blue
2:        0.1537296       saltires
3:        0.1313155  botrightblue
```

```
4:        0.1262545    mainhueblue
5:        0.1205012          nStrp3
6:        0.1149405         quarters
```

The `blue` and `saltires` features define very relevant attributes. In order to visualize the most relevant features, we can build a chart with the top 12 attributes, as shown:

```
dtGainsTop <- dtGains[1:12]
barplot(
  height = dtGainsTop[, attr_importance],
  names.arg = dtGainsTop[, feature],
  main = 'information gain',
  col = rainbow(nrow(dtGainsTop)),
  legend.text = dtGainsTop[, feature],
  xlim=c(0, 20)
)
```

The histogram obtained is as follows:

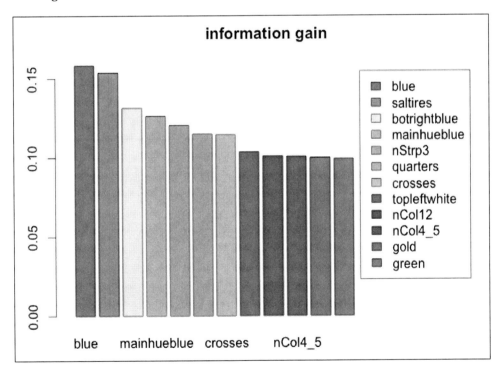

Now that we have defined feature ranking, we are able to build a model from the most relevant features. We can either include all the features whose relevance is above a chosen threshold, or pick a defined number of features starting from the top. However, we are still not taking into account the interaction between the features. For instance, among the top features, we have `the flag contains the blue`, `blue is the main color`, and `the bottom right is blue`. Although they are all very relevant, they are all about `blue`, so they are redundant and we can exclude one of them.

In conclusion, the filters are fast and useful methods to rank the features, but we have to be very careful about using them when we build the model.

# Summary

In this chapter, you learned how to perform feature selection. After having loaded and explored the features, you saw how to transform them using discretization and binarization. You also converted categoric features into dummy variables. You understood the importance of feature selection and ranked the features using the information gain ratio. In the next chapter, we will predict the language using machine learning techniques.

# 5
# Step 2 – Applying Machine Learning Techniques

This chapter focuses on applying the machine learning algorithm, and it is the core of developing the solution. There are different types of techniques that learn from the data. Depending on our target, we can use the data to identify similarities between objects or to estimate an attribute on new objects.

In order to show the machine learning techniques, we start from the flag data that we processed in the previous chapter. However, reading this chapter doesn't require you to know about the previous, although it is recommended to understand where the data came from.

In this chapter you will learn to:

- Identify homogeneous groups of items
- Explore and visualize the item groups
- Estimate a new country language
- Set the configuration of a machine learning technique

# Identifying a homogeneous group of items

Our data describes each country flag. Is there any way to identify groups of countries with similar flag attributes? We can use some clustering techniques that are machine learning algorithms that define homogeneous clusters using the data.

Starting from the flag attributes, in the previous chapter, we built a feature table and we stored it into the `dtFeatures.txt` file. In order to load the file into R, the first step is to define the directory containing the file using `setwd`. Then, we can load the file into the `dfFeatures` data frame using `read.table`, and we can convert it into the `dtFeatures` data table, as shown:

```
# load the flag features
setwd('<INSER YOUR DIRECTORY/PATH>")
dfFeatures <- read.table(file = 'dtFeatures.txt')
library("data.table")
dtFeatures <- data.table(dfFeatures)
```

Let's take a look at the data using `str`, similar to the previous chapters:

```
# explore the features
str(dtFeatures)
Classes 'data.table' and 'data.frame':    194 obs. of  38 variables:
 $ language    : Factor w/ 10 levels "Arabic","Chinese",..: 8 7 1 3
   7 8 3 3 10 10 ...
 $ red         : Factor w/ 2 levels "no","yes": 2 2 2 2 2 2 1 2 1 1
   ...
 $ green       : Factor w/ 2 levels "no","yes": 2 1 2 1 1 1 1 1 1 1
   ...
 $ blue        : Factor w/ 2 levels "no","yes": 1 1 1 2 2 1 2 2 2 2
   ...
```

The language column is a factor and there are 10 languages, called `levels` of the factor. All the other columns contain features describing the flags and they are factors with two levels: `yes` and `no`. The features are as follows:

- The `colors` feature (for example, `red`) has a `yes` level if the flag contains the color

- The `patterns` feature (for example, `circle`) has a `yes` level if the flag contains the pattern

- The `nBars`/`nstrp`/`ncol` features followed by a number (for example, `nBars3`) have a `yes` level if the flag has 3 bars

- The `topleft`/`botright`/`mainhue` features followed by a color (for example, `topleftblue`) have a `yes` level if the top-left part is blue

# Identifying the groups using k-means

Our target is to identify groups of similar flags. For this purpose, we can start using a basic clustering algorithm, that is, **k-means**.

The k-means target is to identify *k* (for example, eight) homogeneous clusters of flags. Imagine dividing all the flags in eight clusters. One of them includes 10 flags out of which seven contain the color red. Let's suppose that we have a red attribute that is 1 if the flag contains red and 0 otherwise. We can say that the average flag of this cluster contains red with a probability of 70 percent, so its red attribute is 0.7. Doing the same with every other attribute, we can define average flag, whose attributes are the average within the group. Each cluster has an average flag that we can determine using the same approach.

The k-means algorithm is based on an average object that is called the cluster center. At the beginning, the algorithm divides the flags into 8 random groups and determines their 8 centers. Then, k-means reassigns each flag to the group whose center is the most similar. In this way, the clusters are more homogeneous and the algorithm can recompute their centers. After a few iterations, we have 8 groups containing homogeneous flags.

The k-means algorithm is a very popular technique and R provides us with the kmeans function. In order to use it, we can take a look at its help:

```
# K-MEANS
# see the function documentation
help(kmeans)
```

We need two inputs:

- x: A numeric data matrix
- centers: The number of clusters (or the cluster centers to start with)

Starting from dtFeatures, we need to build a numeric feature matrix dtFeaturesKm. First, we can put the feature names into arrayFeatures and generate the dtFeaturesKm data table containing all the features. Perform the following steps:

1. Define arrayFeatures that is a vector containing the feature name. The dtFeatures method contains the attribute in the first column and the features in the others, so we extract all the column names apart from the first:

   ```
   arrayFeatures <- names(dtFeatures)[-1]
   ```

2. Define dtFeaturesKm containing the features:

   ```
   dtFeaturesKm <- dtFeatures[, arrayFeatures, with=F]
   ```

3. Convert a generic column (for example, `red`) into the numeric format. We can use `as.numeric` to convert the column format from factor into numeric:

```
dtFeaturesKm[, as.numeric(red)]
```

4. The new vector contains 1 if the value is `no` and 2 if the value is `yes`. In order to use the same standards as our k-means descriptions, we prefer to have 0 if the attribute is `no` and 1 if the attribute is `yes`. In this way, when we are computing the average attribute within a group, it will be a number between 0 and 1 that can be seen as a portion of flags whose attribute is `yes`. Then, in order to have 0 and 1, we can use `as.numeric(red) - 1`:

```
dtFeaturesKm[, as.numeric(red) - 1]
```

Alternatively, we could have done the same using the ifelse function.

5. We need to convert each column format into 0-1. The `arrayFeatures` data table contains names of all the features and we can process each of them using a `for` loop. If we want to transform a column whose name is contained in `nameCol`, we need to use the `eval-get` notation. With `eval(nameCol) :=` we redefine the column, and with `get(nameCol)` we use the current value of the column, as shown:

```
for(nameCol in arrayFeatures)
  dtFeaturesKm[
    , eval(nameCol) := as.numeric(get(nameCol)) - 1
    ]
```

6. Now convert all the features in the 0-1 format. Let's visualize it:

```
View(dtFeaturesKm)
```

7. The `kmeans` function requires the data to be in the matrix form. In order to convert `dtFeaturesKm` into a matrix, we can use `as.matrix`:

```
matrixFeatures <- as.matrix(dtFeaturesKm)
```

The `matrixFeatures` data table contains data to build the k-means algorithm and the other `kmeans` inputs are the parameters. The k-means algorithm doesn't automatically detect the number of clusters, so we need to specify it through the `centers` input. Given the set of objects, we can identify any number of clusters out of them. Which is the number that reflects the data most? There are some techniques that allow us to define it, but they're out of the scope of this chapter. We can just define a reasonable number of centers, for example, 8:

```
# cluster the data using the k-means
nCenters <- 8
modelKm <- kmeans(
  x = matrixFeatures,
```

```
centers = nCenters
)
```

The `modelKm` function is a list containing different model components. The help of `kmeans` provides us with a detailed description of the output and we can use `names` to get the element names. Let's see the components:

```
names(modelKm)
[1] "cluster"      "centers"    "totss"     "withinss"
[5] "tot.withinss" "betweenss"  "size"      "iter"
[9] "ifault"
```

We can visualize the cluster centers that are contained in `centers`, as shown:

```
View(modelKm$centers)
```

Each row defines a center and each column shows an attribute. All the attributes are between 0 and 1, and they represent the percentage of flags in the cluster with an attribute equal to 1. For instance, if `red` is `0.5`, it means that half of the flags contain the color red.

The element that we will use is `cluster` and it contains a label specifying the cluster of each flag. For instance, if the first element of a cluster is `3`, this means that the first flag in `matrixFeatures` (and also in `dtFeatures`) belongs to the third cluster.

# Exploring the clusters

We can take a look at each cluster in order to explore its flags. In order to do that, we can add the cluster to the initial table by defining the `clusterKm` column, as shown:

```
# add the cluster to the data table
dtFeatures[, clusterKm := modelKm$cluster]
```

In order to explore a cluster, we can determine how many of its countries speak each language. Starting from `dtFeatures`, we can summarize the data about each cluster using data table aggregation. First, let's define the column that contains the cluster:

```
# aggregate the data by cluster
nameCluster <- 'clusterKm'
```

We want to determine how many rows we have in each cluster. The data table command that allows us to determine the number of rows is `.N`, shown as follows:

```
dtFeatures[, list(.N), by=nameCluster]
```

If we want to have a different column name for the cluster size, we can specify it within the list, as shown:

```
dtFeatures[, list(nCountries=.N), by=nameCluster]
```

In order to determine how many countries we have for each language, we can use `table`:

```
dtFeatures[, table(language)]
```

In order to use `table` within an aggregation, the output should be a list. For this purpose, we can convert the table using `as.list`, as shown:

```
dtFeatures[, as.list(table(language))]
```

Now, we can apply this operation to each group using `by`, as shown:

```
dtFeatures[, as.list(table(language)), by=nameCluster]
```

What if we want to visualize the percentage of countries speaking each language? We can divide each value of the table by the number of countries in the cluster, as follows:

```
dtFeatures[, as.list(table(language) / .N), by=nameCluster]
```

We want to generate `dtClusters` containing the number of countries in each group and the percentage of each language. In order to do this, we can generate two lists using the commands that we've just seen. In order to combine the two lists, we can just use `c(list1, list2)`, as shown:

```
dtClusters <- dtFeatures[
  , c(list(nCountries=.N), as.list(table(language) / .N)),
  by=nameCluster
  ]
```

Each row of `dtClusters` represents a cluster. The `nCountries` column displays the number of countries in the cluster and all the other columns show the percentage of each language. In order to visualize this data, we can build a histogram with a bar for each cluster. Each bar is divided into segments representing the number of countries speaking each language. The `barplot` function allows us to build the desired chart, if we give a matrix as the input. Each matrix column corresponds to a bar and each row defines the chunks in which the bar is divided.

We need to define a matrix containing the language percentages. This can be done by carrying out the following steps:

1.  Define `arrayLanguages` containing the `dtClusters` language column names:

    ```
    arrayLanguages <- dtFeatures[, unique(language)]
    ```

2.  Build `dtBarplot` containing the language columns:

    ```
    dtBarplot <- dtClusters[, arrayLanguages, with=F]
    ```

3. Convert `dtBarplot` into a matrix using `as.matrix`. In order to build the chart, we need to transpose the matrix (invert the rows and columns) using the R function `t`:

```
matrixBarplot <- t(as.matrix(dtBarplot))
```

4. Define a vector with the cluster sizes, that is, the number of countries. We will display the numbers under the columns:

```
nBarplot <- dtClusters[, nCountries]
```

5. Define the legend names as the country names:

```
namesLegend <- names(dtBarplot)
```

6. Reduce the legend names' length in order to avoid having a legend overlapping the chart. Using `substring`, we limit the names to 12 characters, as shown:

```
help(substring)
namesLegend <- substring(namesLegend, 1, 12)
```

7. Define the colors using `rainbow`. We need to define a color for each element of `namesLegend`, so the number of colors is `length(namesLegend)`, as shown:

```
arrayColors <- rainbow(length(namesLegend))
```

8. Define the chart title using `paste`:

```
plotTitle <- paste('languages in each cluster of', nameCluster)
```

Now we have all the `barplot` inputs, so we can build the chart. In order to be sure that the legend dosen't overlap the bars, we include the `xlim` argument that specifies the plot boundaries, as shown:

```
# build the histogram
barplot(
  height = matrixBarplot,
  names.arg = nBarplot,
  col = arrayColors,
  legend.text = namesLegend,
  xlim = c(0, ncol(matrixBarplot) * 2),
  main = plotTitle,
  xlab = 'cluster'
)
```

The chart obtained is as follows:

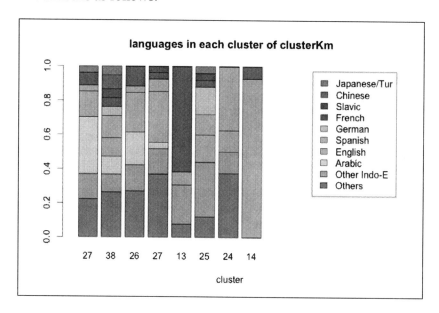

The k-means algorithm performs a series of steps starting from the initial clusters that are defined by splitting the data randomly. The final output depends on the initial random split that is different every time we run the algorithm. So, if we run k-means more than once, we might obtain different results. However, this chart helps us identify some patterns within the language group. For instance, in the eighth cluster, almost all the countries speak English, so we can deduce that there are some English-speaking countries with a similar flag. In the fifth cluster, more than half of the countries speak French, so we can deduce the same. Some less relevant results are that Arabic has a high share in the first cluster and Spanish is quite relevant in the seventh cluster.

We are using other clustering algorithms and we will visualize the results in a similar way. In order to have clean and compact code, we can define the `plotCluster` function. The inputs are the `dtFeatures` feature data table and the `nameCluster` cluster column name. The code is almost the same as the preceding one, shown as follows:

```
# define a function to build the histogram
plotCluster <- function(
  dtFeatures, # data table with the features
  nameCluster # name of the column defining the cluster
){
```

```
# aggregate the data by cluster
dtClusters <- dtFeatures[
  , c(list(nCountries=.N), as.list(table(language) / .N)),
  by=nameCluster]

# prepare the histogram inputs
arrayLanguages <- dtFeatures[, unique(language)]
dtBarplot <- dtClusters[, arrayLanguages, with=F]
matrixBarplot <- t(as.matrix(dtBarplot))
nBarplot <- dtClusters[, nCountries]
namesLegend <- names(dtBarplot)
namesLegend <- substring(namesLegend, 1, 12)
arrayColors <- rainbow(length(namesLegend))

# build the histogram
barplot(
  height = matrixBarplot,
  names.arg = nBarplot,
  col = arrayColors,
  legend.text = namesLegend,
  xlim=c(0, ncol(matrixBarplot) * 2),
  main = paste('languages in each cluster of', nameCluster),
  xlab = 'cluster'
)

}
```

This function should build the same histogram as the previous one. Let's check it using the following code:

```
# visualize the histogram using the functions
plotCluster(dtFeatures, nameCluster)
```

Another way to visualize the clusters is to build a world map using a different color for each cluster. In addition, we can visualize a world map for the languages.

In order to build the map, we need to install and load the `rworldmap` package, as shown:

```
# define a function for visualizing the world map
install.packages('rworldmap')
library(rworldmap)
```

This package builds a world map starting from the country names, that is, in our case the df Features row names. We can add the country column to dtFeatures, as shown:

```
dtFeatures[, country := rownames(dfFeatures)]
```

Our data is quite old so Germany is still divided in two parts. In order to visualize it on the map, we can convert Germany-FRG into Germany. Similarly, we can convert USSR into Russia, as shown:

```
dtFeatures[country == 'Germany-FRG', country := 'Germany']
dtFeatures[country == 'USSR', country := 'Russia']
```

Now, we can define a function to build a world map showing the clusters. The inputs are the dtFeatures data table and the colPlot column name of the feature to visualize (for example, clusterKm). The other argument is colourPalette and it determines the color to be used in the map. See help(mapCountryData) for more information, as shown:

```
plotMap <- function(
  dtFeatures, # data table with the countries
  colPlot # feature to visualize
  colourPalette = 'negpos8' # colors
){
  # function for visualizing a feature on the world map
```

We define the colPlot column containing the cluster to visualize. In the case of a string, we use just the first 12 characters, as shown:

```
# define the column to plot
dtFeatures[, colPlot := NULL]
dtFeatures[, colPlot := substring(get(colPlot), 1, 12)]
```

We build mapFeatures containing the data that we need to build the chart. See help(joinCountryData2Map) for more information. The joinCode = 'NAME' input specifies that the countries are defined by their names and not by an abbreviation. The nameJoinColumn specifies which column we have the country names in, shown as follows:

```
# prepare the data to plot
mapFeatures <- joinCountryData2Map(
  dtFeatures[, c('country', 'colPlot'), with=F],
  joinCode = 'NAME',
  nameJoinColumn = 'country'
)
```

We can build the chart using `mapCountryData`. We specify that we are using the colors of the rainbow and that the country with the missing data will be gray, as shown in the following code:

```
# build the chart
mapCountryData(
  mapFeatures,
  nameColumnToPlot='colPlot',
  catMethod = 'categorical',
  colourPalette = colourPalette,
  missingCountryCol = 'gray',
  mapTitle = colPlot
)

}
```

Now, we can use `plotMap` to visualize the k-means clusters on the world map, as shown:

```
plotMap(dtFeatures, colPlot = 'clusterKm')
```

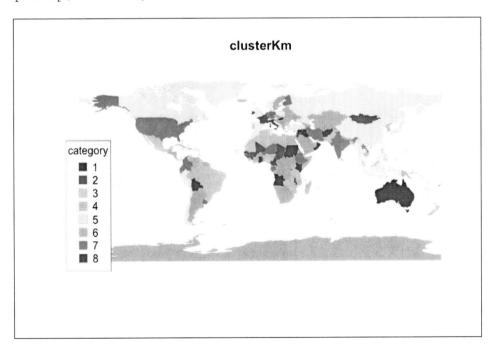

We can see that many Asian countries belong to the fifth cluster. In addition, we can observe that Italy, France, and Ireland belong to the same cluster, since their flag is similar. Apart from that, it's hard to identify any other pattern.

# Identifying a cluster's hierarchy

Other techniques to identify homogeneous groups are the hierarchic clustering algorithms. These techniques build the clusters, merging the objects iteratively. At the beginning, we have a cluster for each country. We define a measure of how *similar* two clusters are and, at each step, we identify the two clusters whose flag is the most *similar* and merge them into a unique cluster. In the end, we have a cluster including all the countries.

The R function that performs hierarchic clustering is `hclust`. Let's take a look at its `help` function:

```
# HIERARCHIC CLUSTERING
# function for hierarchic clustering
help(hclust)
```

The first input is `d` and the documentation explains that it's a dissimilarity structure, that is, a matrix containing all the distances between the objects. As suggested by the documentation, we can use the `dist` function to build the input, as shown:

```
# build the distance matrix
help(dist)
```

The input of `dist` is a numeric matrix describing the flags. We already built `matrixDistances` for the k-means algorithm, so we can reuse it. The other relevant input is `method` and it specifies how `dist` measures the distance between two flags. Which method should we use? All the features are binary as they have two possible outcomes, that is, `0` and `1`. Then, the distance can be the number of attributes with a different value. The `method` object that determines the distance in this way is `manhattan`, as shown:

```
matrixDistances <- dist(matrixFeatures, method = 'manhattan')
```

The `matrixDistances` function contains the dissimilarity between any two flags. The other input is `method` and it specifies the agglomeration method. In our case, we set the method as `complete`. There are other options for `method` and they define the linkage, that is, the way of computing the distance between clusters, as shown:

```
# build the hierarchic clustering model
modelHc <- hclust(d = matrixDistances, method = 'complete')
```

The `modelHc` method contains the clustering model and we can visualize the cluster using `plot`. You can consult the help of `hclust` to understand the `plot` parameters, as shown:

```
# visualize the hierarchic clustering model
plot(modelHc, labels = FALSE, hang = -1)
```

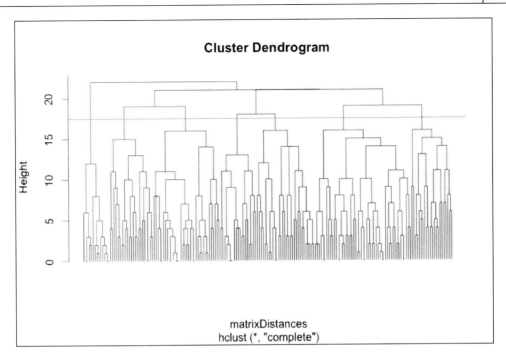

This chart shows the algorithm procedure. At the bottom, we have all the countries, and each flag belongs to a different cluster. Each line represents a cluster and the lines converge when the algorithm merges the clusters. On the left-hand side of the chart, you can see a scale representing the distance between the flags, and at each level the algorithm merges the clusters that are at a specific distance from each other. At the top, all the flags belong to the same cluster. This chart is called **dendrogram**. Consider the following code:

```
# define the clusters
heightCut <- 17.5
abline(h=heightCut, col='red')
```

The clusters that we want to identify are the ones above the red line. The function that identifies the cluster starting from modelHc is cutree, and we can specify the horizontal line height in the h argument, as shown:

```
cutree(modelHc, h = heightCut)
```

Now, we can add the cluster to dtFeatures, as shown:

```
dcFeatures[, clusterHc := cutree(modelHc, h = heightCut)]
```

As mentioned earlier, we can see which languages are spoken in each cluster. We can reuse `plotCluster` and `plotMap`:

```
# visualize the clusters
plotCluster(dtFeatures, nameCluster = 'clusterHc')
```

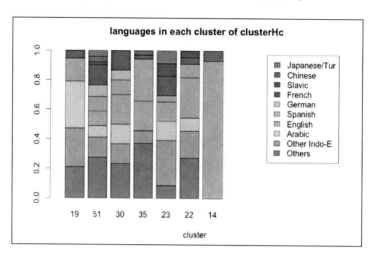

In the eighth cluster, English is the predominant language. Apart from that, Arabic is relevant in the first cluster only, French and German are relevant in the second and third if taken together, and Spanish is relevant in the third.

We can also visualize the world map with the clusters, as shown:

```
plotMap(dtFeatures, colPlot = 'clusterHc')
```

The chart obtained is as follows:

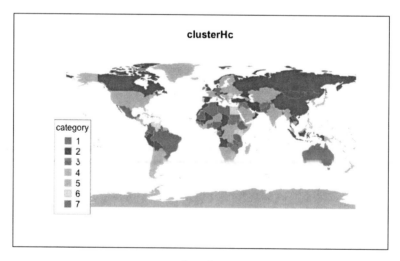

Similar to k-means, the only continent with a predominant cluster is Asia.

This section described two popular clustering techniques that identify homogeneous flag clusters. They both allow us to understand the similarities between different flags, and we can use this information as support to solve some problems.

# Applying the k-nearest neighbor algorithm

This section shows you how to estimate a new country language starting from its flag, using a simple supervised learning technique that is the **k-nearest neighbor (KNN)**. In this case, we estimate the language, which is a `categoric` attribute so we use a classification technique. If the attribute was numeric, we would have used a regression technique. The reason I chose KNN is that it's simple to explain, and there are some options to modify its parameters in order to improve the result's accuracy.

Let's see how the KNN works. We know the flag and the language of 150 countries and we want to determine the language of a new country starting from its flag. First, we identify the 10 countries whose flag is the most similar to the new one. Out of them, we have six Spanish-speaking countries, two English-speaking countries, one French-speaking country, and one Arabic-speaking country.

Out of these 10 countries, the most common language is Spanish, so we can expect that the new flag belongs to a Spanish-speaking country.

The KNN is based upon this approach. In order to estimate a new country language, we identify the *K* countries whose flag is the most similar. Then, we estimate that the new country speaks the most common language among them.

We have a table describing 194 flags through 37 binary attributes whose value can be `Yes` or `No`. For instance, the `mainhuegreen` attribute is `yes`, if the predominant flag color is green and `no` otherwise. All the attributes describe the flag's colors and patterns.

Similar to the previous section, before modifying `dtFeatures`, we define `arrayFeatures` containing the feature names. As we added some columns to `dtFeatures`, we extract the feature names from `dfFeatures`. Then, we add the `country` column with the country names coming from `dfFeatures`, as shown:

```
# define the feature names
arrayFeatures <- names(dfFeatures)[-1]
# add the country to dtFeatures
dtFeatures[, country := rownames(dfFeatures)]
dtFeatures[country == 'Germany-FRG', country := 'Germany']
dtFeatures[country == 'USSR', country := 'Russia']
```

Starting from dtFeatures, we can apply KNN. Given a new flag, how do we determine which are the 10 most similar flags? Given any two flags, we can measure how *similar* they are. The easiest way is to count how many features have the same value across the two flags. The more attributes they have in common, the more similar they are.

In the previous chapter, we already explored and transformed the features, so we don't need to process them. However, we haven't explored the language column yet. For each language, we can determine how many countries speak the language using table, as shown:

```
dtFeatures[, table(language)]
```

The number of countries varies a lot from one language to another. The most popular language is English, with 43 countries, and there are some languages with just four countries. In order to have an overview of all the languages, we can visualize the table by building a chart. In the previous section, we defined plotMap, which shows the groups on the world map. We can use it to show the countries speaking each language, as shown:

```
plotMap(dtFeatures, colPlot = 'language', colourPalette =
    'rainbow')
```

The chart obtained is as follows:

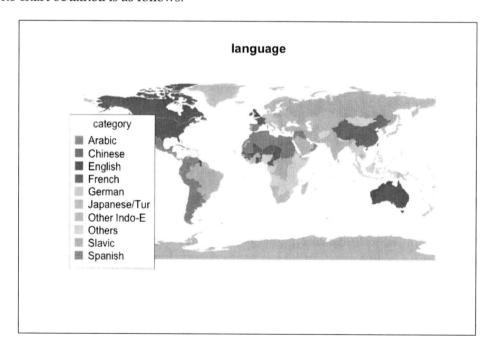

It's nice to see a map showing countries that speak each language, but it's still a bit hard to understand how big the groups are. A better option is to generate a pie chart whose slices are proportional to the number of countries in each group. The R function is `pie`, as shown:

```
# visualize the languages
help(pie)
```

The `pie` function requires an input, that is, a vector containing the number of countries speaking each language. If the input vector fields have a name, it'll be displayed in the chart. We can build the required vector using `table`, as shown:

```
arrayTable <- dtFeatures[, table(language)]
```

Fortunately, `pie` doesn't require any other argument:

```
pie(arrayTable)
```

The chart obtained is as follows:

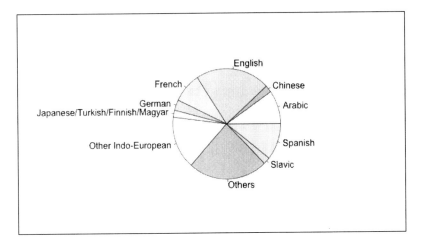

There are some languages that are spoken in just a few countries. For instance, there are just 4 Slavic countries. Given a new country, we want to determine its language starting from its flag. Let's pretend that we don't know which language is spoken in one of the 4 Slavic countries. If we take into account its 10 nearest neighbors, there cannot be more than 3 other Slavic countries. What if there are 4 English-speaking countries out of its 10 neighbors? Despite all the remaining Slavic countries that are in its neighborhood, there are more English countries just because the English group is bigger. Therefore, the algorithm will estimate that the country is English. Similarly, we have the same issue with any other small group. Like almost all the machine learning algorithm, the KNN won't be able to classify the countries that belong to any other smaller group.

While dealing with any classification problem, if some groups are small, we don't have enough related information. In this context, even a good technique won't be able to classify the new objects that belong to a small group. In addition, given a new country that belongs to a medium-sized group, it likely has a lot of neighbors that belong to the big groups. Therefore, a new country speaking one of these languages might be assigned to the big groups.

By knowing the model limitations, we can define a feasible machine learning problem. In order to avoid having small groups, we can merge some groups. The clustering techniques allowed us to identify which language groups are more well-defined, and accordingly, we can split the languages in these groups: English, Spanish, French and German, Slavic and other Indo-European, Arabic, and Other.

We can define the language groups to build listGroups whose elements contain the language spoken by the groups. For instance, we can define the indoEu group containing Slavic and Other Indo-European language, as shown:

```
# reduce the number of groups
listGroups <- list(
  english = 'English',
  spanish = 'Spanish',
  frger = c('French', 'German'),
  indoEu = c('Slavic', 'Other Indo-European'),
  arabic = 'Arabic',
  other = c(
    'Japanese/Turkish/Finnish/Magyar', 'Chinese', 'Others'
    )
  )
```

Now, we can redefine the language column containing the language groups. For each element of listGroups, we convert all the languages into the element name. For instance, we convert Slavic and Other Indo-European into indoEu.

We can perform this operation within a `for` loop. All the group names are contained in the list names, so we can iterate over the elements of `names(listGroups)`, as shown:

```
for(nameGroup in names(listGroups)){
```

Here, `nameGroup` defines a group name and `listGroups[[nameGroup]]` contains its languages. We can extract the rows of `dtFeatures` speaking any of the group languages, using `language %in% listGroups[[nameGroup]]`. Then, we can reassign the language column to the `nameGroup` group name using the `:=` data table notation, as shown:

```
dtFeatures[
    language %in% listGroups[[nameGroup]],
    language := nameGroup
    ]
}
```

We redefined the `language` column grouping the languages. Let's take a look at it:

```
dtFeatures[, language]
```

Here, `language` is a factor and there are just six possible levels that are our language groups. However, you can see that R has printed `16 Levels: Arabic Chinese English French ... Other` in the console. The reason is that the `language` column format is `factor` and it keeps track of the 10 initial values. In order to display just the six language groups, we can redefine the `language` column using `factor`, as shown:

```
dtFeatures[, language := factor(language)]
dtFeatures[, language]
```

Now we have just six levels. Just like we did earlier, we can visualize the group sizes data using `plotMap`, as shown:

```
# visualize the language groups
plotMap(dtFeatures, colPlot = 'language')
```

The map obtained is as follows:

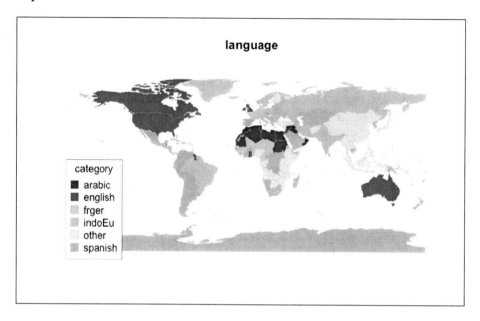

We can see that the countries of each category are geographically close to each other.

In order to visualize the new group sizes, we can use `pie`, as shown:

```
pie(dtFeatures[, table(language)])
```

The chart obtained is as follows:

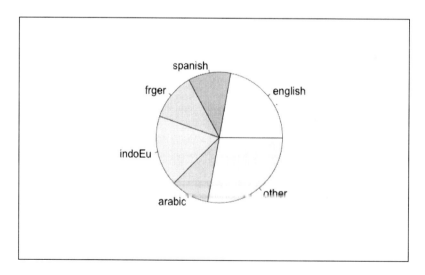

All the six groups contain enough countries. The **english** and **other** groups are a bit bigger than the others, but the sizes are comparable.

Now we can build the KNN model. R provides us with the kknn package containing the KNN algorithm. Let's install and load the package, as shown:

```
# install and load the package
install.packages("kknn")
library(kknn)
```

The function that builds the KNN is called kknn, such as the package. Let's see its help function:

```
help(kknn)
```

The first input is formula and it defines the features and the output. Then, we have to define a training set, containing the data to be used to build the model, and a test set, containing the data upon which we are applying the model. We use all the information about the training set and pretend not to know the language of the test set countries. There are other optional inputs defining some model parameters.

All the feature names are contained in arrayFeatures. In order to define how the output depends on the features, we need to build a string in the output ~ feature1 + feature2 + .... format. Perform the following steps:

1. Define the first part of the string: output ~ :

   ```
   formulaKnn <- 'language ~'
   ```

2. For each feature, add + feature using paste:

   ```
   for(nameFeature in arrayFeatures){
      formulaKnn <- paste(formulaKnn, '+', nameFeature)
   }
   ```

3. Convert the string into the formula format:

   ```
   formulaKnn <- formula(formulaKnn)
   ```

We built formulaKnn containing the relationship to put into kknn.

Now, we need to define the training set and the test set starting from dtFeatures. A fair split is putting 80 percent of the data in the training set, and for this purpose we can add each country to the training set with a probability of 80 percent and to the test set otherwise. We can define the indexTrain vector whose length is equal to the number of lines in dtFeatures. The R function is sample, as shown:

```
help(sample)
```

The arguments are:

- x: The values to be put into the vector that are TRUE and FALSE in this case.
- size: The length of the vector that is the number of rows in dtFeatures in our case.
- replace: In order to sample the values more than once, it's TRUE.
- prob: The probability of choosing the elements of x. In our case, we pick TRUE with a probability of 80 percent and FALSE with a probability of 20 percent.

Using our arguments, we can build indexTrain, shown as follows:

```
# split the dataset into training and test set
indexTrain <- sample(
  x=c(TRUE, FALSE),
  size=nrow(dtFeatures),
  replace=TRUE,
  prob=c(0.8, 0.2)
)
```

Now, we need to add the rows, for which indexTrain is TRUE, to the training set and the remaining rows to the testing set. We extract all the rows, for which indexTrain is TRUE, using a simple data table operation, as shown:

```
dtTrain <- dtFeatures[indexTrain]
```

In order to extract the test rows, we have to switch TRUE and FALSE using the NOT operator that in R is !, as shown:

```
dtTest <- dtFeatures[!indexTrain]
```

Now we have all the basic arguments for using kknn. The other parameters that we set are:

- k: The number of neighbors is 10.
- kernel: KNN has the option of assigning a different relevance to the features, but we're not using this feature at the moment. Setting the kernel parameter as rectangular, we use the basic KNN.
- distance: We want to compute the distance between two flags as the number of attributes that they don't have in common (similar to the previous chapter). In order to do this, we set the distance parameter equal to 1. For more information, you can learn about **Minkowski distance**.

Let's build the KNN model:

```
# build the model
modelKnn <- kknn(
  formula = formulaKnn,
  train = dtTrain,
  test = dtTest,
  k = 10,
  kernel = 'rectangular',
  distance = 1
)
```

The model has learned from `dtTrain` and estimated the language of the countries in `dtTest`. As we can see in the `kknn` help, `modelKnn` is a list containing a description of the model. The component showing the predicted language is `fitted.valued`, as shown:

```
# extract the fitted values
modelKnn$fitted.values
```

We can add the predicted language to `dtTest` in order to compare it with the real language:

```
# add the estimated language to dtTest
dtTest[, languagePred := modelKnn$fitted.values]
```

For the countries in `dtTest`, we know the real and the predicted languages. We can count how many times they are the same using `sum(language == languagePred)`. We can measure the model accuracy by dividing the number of correct predictions by the total, that is, `.N` (the number of rows), as shown:

```
# evaluate the model
percCorrect <- dtTest[, sum(language == languagePred) / .N]
percCorrect
```

Here, `percCorrect` varies a lot depending on the training/test dataset split. As we have different language groups, `percCorrect` is not particularly high.

# Optimizing the k-nearest neighbor algorithm

We built our KNN model using 37 features that have a different relevance to the language. Given a new flag, its neighbors are the flags sharing a lot of attributes, regardless of their relevance. If a flag has different common attributes that are irrelevant to the language, we erroneously include it in the neighborhood. On the other hand, if a flag shares a few highly-relevant attributes, it won't be included.

KNN performs worse in the presence of irrelevant attributes. This fact is called the curse of dimensionality and it's quite common in machine learning algorithms. A solution to the curse of dimensionality is to rank the features on the basis of their relevance and to select the most relevant. Another option that we won't see in this chapter is using dimensionality reduction techniques.

In the previous chapter, in the *Ranking the features using a filter or a dimensionality reduction* section, we measured the feature's relevance using the information gain ratio. Now, we can compute the dtGains table, similar to the previous chapter, starting from dtTrain. We cannot use the whole dtFeatures because we're pretending not to know the language of the test set countries. If you want to see how information.gain works, you can take a look at *Chapter 4, Step 1 – Data Exploration and Feature Engineering*. Consider the following example:

```
# compute the information gain ratio
library('FSelector')
formulaFeat <- paste(arrayFeatures, collapse = ' + ')
formulaGain <- formula(paste('language', formulaFeat, sep = ' ~ '))
dfGains <- information.gain(language~., dtTrain)
dfGains$feature <- row.names(dfGains)
dtGains <- data.table(dfGains)
dtGains <- dtGains[order(attr_importance, decreasing = T)]
View(dtGains)
```

The feature column contains the feature names and the attr_importance column displays the feature gain, which expresses its relevance. In order to select the most relevant features, we can first rebuild arrayFeatures with the sorted features. Then, we'll be able to select the top, as shown:

```
# re-define the feature vector
arrayFeatures <- dtGains[, feature]
```

Starting from `arrayFeatures` and given a `nFeatures` number, we want to build the formula using the top `nFeatures` features. In order to be able to do this for any `nFeatures`, we can define a function to build the formula, as shown:

```
# define a function for building the formula
buildFormula <- function(
  arrayFeatures, # feature vector
  nFeatures # number of features to include
){
```

The steps are as follows:

1. Extract the top `nFeatures` features and put them into `arrayFeaturesTop`:

   ```
   arrayFeaturesTop <- arrayFeatures[1:nFeatures]
   ```

2. Build the first part of the formula string:

   ```
   formulaKnn <- paste('language', '~')
   ```

3. Add the features to the formula:

   ```
   for(nameFeature in arrayFeaturesTop){
      formulaKnn <- paste(formulaKnn, '+', nameFeature)
   }
   ```

4. Convert `formulaKnn` into a `formula` format:

   ```
   formulaKnn <- formula(formulaKnn)
   ```

5. Return the output:

   ```
      return(formulaKnn)
   }
   ```

Using our function, we can build `formulaKnnTop` using the top 10 features, as shown:

```
formulaKnnTop <- buildFormula(arrayFeatures, nFeatures = 10)
formulaKnnTop
```

Now, we can build the model using the same inputs as before, with the exception of `formula` input that now contains `formulaKnnTop`, as shown:

```
# build the model
modelKnn <- kknn(
  formula = formulaKnnTop,
  train = dtTrain,
  test = dtTest,
  k = 10,
  kernel = 'rectangular',
  distance = 1
)
```

As mentioned earlier, we can add the predicted language to `dtTest` in a new column called `languagePred10`:

```
# add the output to dtTest
dtTest[, languagePredTop := modelKnn$fitted.values]
```

We can compute the percentage of languages that we identified correctly:

```
# evaluate the model
percCorrectTop <- dtTest[, sum(language == languagePredTop) / .N]
percCorrectTop
```

Have we achieved any improvement by selecting the top features? In order to determine which model is the most accurate, we can compare `percCorrect10` with `percCorrect` and determine which is the highest. We randomly defined the split between `dtTrain` and `dtTest`, so the result changes every time we run the algorithm.

There is another option to avoid the curse of dimensionality. The flags are described by 37 features with different relevancies and we selected the 10 most relevant. In this way, the similarity depends on the number of features that are in common out of the top 10. What if we have two flags with just two out of the top 10 features and 20 out of the remaining features in common? Are they less similar than two flags with three out of the top 10 features in common? Instead of ignoring the other 27 features, we can use them giving them a lower relevance.

There is a KNN variation, called **weighted KNN**, which identifies the relevance of each feature and builds the KNN accordingly. There are different KNN versions and the `kknn` function allows us to use some of them, specifying the `kernel` argument. In our case, we can set `kernel = 'optimal'`, as shown:

```
# build the weighted knn model
modelKnn <- kknn(
  formula = formulaKnn,
  train = dtTrain,
  test = dtTest,
  k = 10,
  kernel = 'optimal',
  distance = 1
)
```

As mentioned earlier, we can measure the accuracy:

```
# add the estimated language to dtTest
dtTest[, languagePredWeighted := modelKnn$fitted.values]
percCorrectWeighted <- dtTest[
  , sum(language == languagePredWeighted) / .N
  ]
```

Depending on the training/test split, `percCorrectWeighted` can be higher or lower than `percCorrect`.

We saw different options to build a supervised machine learning model. In order to identify which performs best, we need to evaluate each option and optimize the parameters.

# Summary

In this chapter, you learned how to identify homogeneous clusters and visualize the clustering process and results. You defined a feasible supervised machine learning problem and solved it using KNN. You evaluated the model, accuracy and modified its parameters. You also ranked the features and selected the most relevant.

In the next chapter, you will see a better approach to evaluating the accuracy of a supervised learning model. You will see a structured approach to optimizing the model parameters and selecting the most relevant features.

# Step 3 – Validating the Results

In the previous chapter, we estimated the language of new countries starting from their flag. For this purpose, we used KNN algorithm that is a supervised learning algorithm. We built KNN and measured its accuracy cross validating the estimated language. In this chapter, we will see how to measure the accuracy in a more reliable way and we will tune the KNN parameters to improve its performance. To be able to do the tasks in this chapter, it's not necessary for you to have read the previous chapter, although it is recommended so that you can order to understand how the KNN algorithm works.

In this chapter, you will learn how to:

- Validate the accuracy of an algorithm
- Tune the algorithm parameters
- Select the most relevant data features
- Optimize the parameters and the features together

## Validating a machine learning model

Starting from a table describing the countries, flags and their language, the KNN estimates a new country language starting from its flag attributes. In this chapter, we will evaluate the performance of KNN.

# Measuring the accuracy of an algorithm

We have already evaluated the algorithm accuracy by cross validating the estimated language. First, we split the data in two parts that are the training set and the test set. Then, we built the KNN algorithm using the training set in order to estimate the test set countries' language. Counting how many times the estimated language was correct, we defined an accuracy index as the percentage of correct guesses. The accuracy depends on which data we put into the test set. Since we randomly defined the training set countries, the accuracy changes every time we repeat the cross validation. Then, the result of this approach is not reliable.

The target of this chapter is to evaluate KNN using a reliable technique in the sense that the accuracy doesn't change validating the same model twice. Repeating the train/set split and the validation many times, almost every country will be in both the training and the test set at least once. We can compute the average accuracy and it will take account of all the countries in both the training and the test sets. After a few iterations, the average accuracy will be reliable since it won't significantly change increasing the number of iterations.

Before evaluating KNN, we need to load the `kknn` and `data.table` packages:

```
# load the packages
library('kknn')
library('data.table')
```

We can define a function building and cross validating KNN using a defined set of parameters and data so that we can quickly evaluate the algorithm with any configuration. Since the R commands are similar to the previous chapter, we will go quickly through them. The input of the functions is:

- A table containing the data
- A vector containing the name of the features that we use
- KNN parameters

The steps are as follows:

1.  Define which rows belong to the training and test sets. We build `indexTrain`, which is a vector specifying which rows will be in the training set. We set a probability of 10 percent for a flag to be in the test set. In *Chapter 5, Step 2 – Applying Machine Learning Techniques*, we set a probability of 20 percent, but in this chapter we will repeat the validation many times, so 10 percent is enough.

2. Starting from `indexTrain`, extract the rows going into `dtTrain` and into `dtTest`.

3. Define the formula defining the features and the attribute to predict.

4. Build KNN using the input parameters.

5. Define the `languageFitted` vector containing the estimated language of the test set.

6. Count how many times `languageFitted` is the same as the real language.

7. Compute the accuracy index as the number of times the predicted language and the real language match, divided by the number of countries in the test set.

This is the R code to build the function. The comments reflect the numbered bullet points, as shown:

```
validateKnn <- function(
  dtFeatures, # data table with the features
  arrayFeatures, # feature names array
  k = 10, # knn parameter
  kernel = 'rectangular', # knn parameter
  distance = 1 # knn parameter
){

  # 1 define the training/test set rows
  indexTrain <- sample(
    x=c(TRUE, FALSE),
    size=nrow(dtFeatures),
    replace=TRUE,
    prob=c(0.9, 0.1)
  )

  # 2 define the training/test set
  dtTrain <- dtFeatures[indexTrain]
  dtTest <- dtFeatures[!indexTrain]

  # 3 define the formula
  formulaOutput <- 'language ~'
  formulaFeatures <- paste(arrayFeatures, collapse = ' + ')
  formulaKnn <- paste(formulaOutput, formulaFeatures)
  formulaKnn <- formula(formulaKnn)
```

```
# 4 build the KNN model
modelKnn <- kknn(
  formula = formulaKnn,
  train = dtTrain,
  test = dtTest,
  k = k,
  kernel = kernel,
  distance = distance
)

# 5 defining the predicted language
languageFitted <- modelKnn$fitted.values

# 6 count the corrected predictions and the total
languageReal <- dtTest[, language]
nRows <- length(languageReal)

# 7 define the accuracy index
percCorrect <- sum(languageFitted == languageReal) / nRows

return(percCorrect)
}
```

Here, `validateKnn` is the starting point to validate the KNN algorithm.

# Defining the average accuracy

In order to use `validateKnn`, we need to define the input, as follows:

- The data table with the features, as shown:

```
setwd('<INSER/YOUR/DIRECTORY/PATH>")
dfFeatures <- read.table(file = 'dtFeatures.txt')
```

- The vector containing all the possible features to include in KNN:

```
arrayFeatures <- names(dfFeatures)
arrayFeatures <- arrayFeatures[arrayFeatures != 'language']
```

- The KNN parameters that can either be set or left as their defaults.

Now, we have all the elements to be able to use `validateKnn`. We can use a random subset of them, for instance, the first 10 features. With regard to the parameters, we can leave all of them to their default, except `k` that is equal to `8`, as shown:

```
# evaluate a model accuracy
validateKnn(
  dtFeatures = dtFeatures,
  arrayFeatures = arrayFeatures[1:10],
  k = 8
)
[1] 0.3571429
```

Running `validateKnn` more than once, we can notice that the result changes every time, as expected. However, now we can define another function running `validateKnn` multiple times. Then, we compute the accuracy average and use it as a reliable performance index. Our new function is called `cvKnn` because it cross validates KNN a defined number of times.

The `cvKnn` arguments are the data table, the number of iterations, the feature names, and the KNN parameters. Let's start defining the data table and the number of iterations. All the other input is the same as `validateKnn`. In order to have clear and compact code, we can use the ellipsis (...) specifying that we can add other arguments. Then, we can pass these arguments to any function using the ellipsis again. This means that when we will call `validateKnn`, we can use `validateKnn(...)` to specify that any extra argument of `cvKnn` will be an input for `validateKnn`.

The function steps are:

1. Defining an empty vector `arrayPercCorrect` that will contain the accuracies.

2. Running `validateKnn` and defining `arrayPercCorrect`, which contains the accuracy.

3. Adding the accuracy `arrayPercCorrect` to `arrayPercCorrect`.

This is the code that builds the function:

```
cvKnn <- function(
  dtFeatures, # data table with the features
  nIterations=10, # number of iterations
  ... # feature names array and knn parameters
){
```

```
# 1 initialize the accuracy array
arrayPercCorrect <- c()

for(iIteration in 1:nIterations){

  # 2 build and validate the knn
  percCorrect <- validateKnn(dtFeatures, ...)

  # 3 add the accuracy to the array
  arrayPercCorrect <- c(arrayPercCorrect, percCorrect)
}

  return(arrayPercCorrect)
}
```

Now, we can use `cvKnn` to build and validate KNN 500 times. Then, we compute the average accuracy as a KNN performance index:

```
# determine the accuracies
arrayPercCorrect = cvKnn(
  dtFeatures, nIterations=500,
  arrayFeatures=arrayFeatures
)
# compute the average accuracy
percCorrectMean <- mean(arrayPercCorrect)
percCorrectMean
[1] 0.2941644
```

We define `percCorrectMean`, which can be used as an accuracy index.

# Visualizing the average accuracy computation

In order to see how much the result changed at any iteration, we can compare each step's accuracy with their average. First, we build a chart with the accuracies using `plot` and the parameters are:

- x: This is the vector that we want to plot (`arrayPercCorrect`).
- ylim: This is the accuracy that is a number between 0 and 1. With `ylim = c(0, 1)`, we specify that the region that we visualize is between 0 and 1.
- xlab and ylab: These are the axis labels.
- main: This is the title.

The code is as follows:

```
# plot the accuracy at each iteration
plot(
  x = arrayPercCorrect,
  ylim = c(0, 1),
  xlab = 'Iteration', ylab = 'Accuracy',
  main = 'Accuracy at each iteration'
)
```

In order to compare the accuracies with their average, we can display the average by drawing a red dashed horizontal line with `abline`, as shown:

```
help(abline)
abline(h=percCorrectMean, col='red', lty='dashed')
```

We can visualize the values' range by drawing a horizontal line for both the minimum and the maximum range, as shown:

```
abline(h=min(arrayPercCorrect), col='blue', lty='dashed')
abline(h=max(arrayPercCorrect), col='blue', lty='dashed')
```

The plot obtained is as follows:

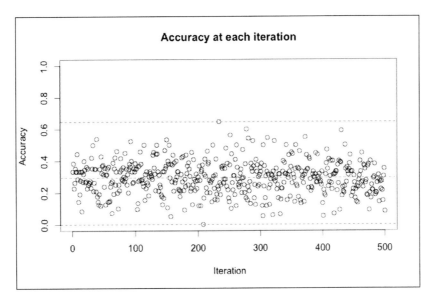

The accuracy varies a lot from one iteration to another and the range is between 0 percent and 70 percent. As expected, a single accuracy is completely unreliable. What about the average among 500 iterations? How many iterations do we need to have a stable result?

We can visualize the accuracy index at the first iteration, then the average among the first two iterations, then the average among the first three, and so on. If at any point the average stops changing, we don't need to go any further. By building a chart we can observe how many iterations it takes to reach a stable average.

First, let's define `arrayCumulate` containing the cumulated average that is the partial average until each iteration, as shown:

```
# plot the average accuracy until each iteration
arrayCumulate <- c()
for(nIter in 1:length(arrayPercCorrect)){
  cumulateAccuracy <- mean(arrayPercCorrect[1:nIter])
  arrayCumulate <- c(arrayCumulate, cumulateAccuracy)
}
```

Using the same commands as before, we build a new chart. The only new argument is `type='l'` and it specifies that we display a line instead of points. In order to zoom into the area with the averages, we remove the `ylim` argument, as shown:

```
plot(
  x = arrayCumulate,
  type = 'l',
  xlab = 'Iteration', ylab = 'Cumulate accuracy',
  main = 'Average accuracy until each iteration'
)
abline(h = percCorrectMean, col = 'red', lty = 'dashed')
```

The plot obtained is as follows:

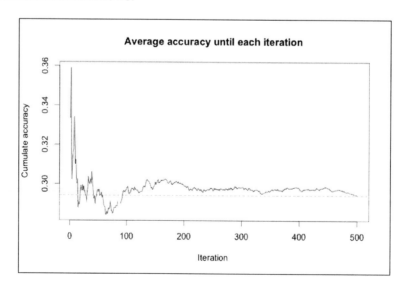

We can notice that the accuracy is nearly stable after the 100 iterations. Assuming that it won't change too much with different parameter configuration, we can use 100 iterations to validate the KNN algorithm.

In this section, we have seen how to automatically evaluate a model performance using a specific set of features and some defined parameters. In the following sections, we will use this function to optimize the model's performance.

# Tuning the parameters

This section shows you how to improve the performance of KNN by tuning its parameters. We are dealing with the $k$ parameter that defines the number of neighbors. Use these steps to identify the $k$ parameter performing best:

1. Define which values of $k$ we will test. The KNN works locally, in the sense that given a new country flag it identifies just a few similar flags. How many of them should we use at most? Since there are less than 200 flags in total, we don't want to use more than 50 flags. Then, we should test each $k$ between 1 and 50 and we can define arrayK containing the options:

   ```
   # define the k to test
   arrayK <- 1:50
   ```

2. Define the number of iterations. For each $k$ in arrayK, we need to build and validate the KNN a sufficiently high amount of times defined by nIterations. In the previous chapter, we learned that we need at least 100 iterations to have a meaningful KNN accuracy:

   ```
   nIterations <- 100
   ```

3. Evaluate the accuracy for each $k$.

4. Choose the $k$ that maximizes the accuracy.

The last two steps are more detailed and we will explore them in depth.

In order to measure the accuracy for each $k$, we define dtAccuracyK as an empty data table that will contain the accuracies. Then, we use a for loop to run KNN with each $k$ in *arrayK* and add the new results. The steps are as follows:

1. Run and validate KNN using cvKnn.

2. Define the rows that we will add to dtAccuracyK containing the accuracy and the $k$.

3. Add the new rows to `dtAccuracyK` using `rbind`:

```
# validate the knn with different k
dtAccuracyK <- data.table()
for(k in arrayK)
{

  # run the KNN and compute the accuracies
  arrayAccuracy <- cvKnn(
    dtFeatures,
    nIterations=nIterations,
    arrayFeatures = arrayFeatures,
    k = k
  )
  # define the new data table rows
  rowsAccuracyK <- data.table(
    accuracy = arrayAccuracy,
    k = k
  )
  # add the new rows to the accuracy table
  dtAccuracyK <- rbind(
    dtAccuracyK,
    rowsAccuracyK
  )
}
```

Now, let's take a look at `result.head(dtAccuracyK)`:

```
   accuracy k
1: 0.3636364 1
2: 0.4545455 1
3: 0.4000000 1
4: 0.2727273 1
5: 0.3000000 1
6: 0.2500000 1
```

Each row of `dtAccuracyK` contains an iteration of KNN. The first column displays the accuracy and the second column displays the *k* used in the iteration.

In order to visualize the results, we can use `plot`. The two dimensions that we want to visualize are the *k* and the accuracy. The input is as follows:

- x, y: These are the plot dimensions that are the k and `accuracy` columns
- `xlab`, `ylab`: These are the axis labels that are k and `accuracy`

- `main`: This is the chart title
- `ylim`: These are the *y* region limits that are `0` and `1`
- `col`: This is the color of the points that is gray, in order to put emphasis on the black points that we will add later

The code is as follows:

```
# plot all the accuracies
plot(
  x = dtAccuracyK[, k],
  y = dtAccuracyK[, accuracy],
  xlab = 'K', ylab = 'Accuracy',
  main = 'KNN accuracy using different k',
  ylim = c(0, 1),
  col = 'grey'
)
```

The plot obtained is as follows:

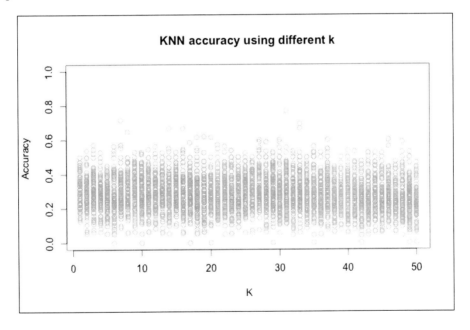

We cannot notice any relevant difference depending on *k*. The reason is that the accuracy varies a lot from one iteration to another. In order to identify *k* performing better, we can compute the average performance for each *k*. We call the new data table dtCvK because we're cross validating the model, as shown:

```
# compute the average accuracy
dtCvK <- dtAccuracyK[
  , list(accuracy = mean(accuracy)),
  by='k'
  ]
View(dtCvK)
```

Here, dtCvK contains the average accuracy of each *k*. We can add it to the chart using points that is a function adding the new points to the current chart. In order to make the points more visible, we display full points using pch = 16, as shown:

```
# add the average accuracy to the chart
help(points)
points(
  x = dtCvK[, k],
  y = dtCvK[, accuracy],
  pch = 16
)
```

The plot is as follows:

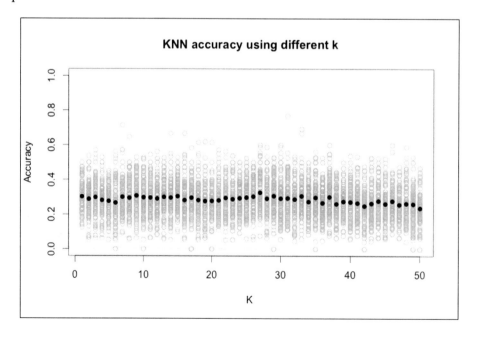

The average accuracies vary across the *k*, but it is hard to notice the difference because it is always around 0.3 to 0.4. In order to see the difference more clearly, we can plot just the average without visualizing the *y* limits, as shown:

```
# plot the average accuracy
plot(
  x = dtCvK[, k],
  y = dtCvK[, accuracy],
  xlab = 'k', ylab = 'accuracy',
  main = 'average knn accuracy using different k',
  type = 'o'
)
```

You can also use `type = 'str(dtCvK)'` instead of `type = 'o'`.

We can identify the *k* performing best and add it to the chart using `abline`:

```
# identify the k performing best
kOpt <- dtCvK[accuracy == max(accuracy), k]
abline(v = kOpt, col = 'red')
```

You can also use `kOpt <- 27` instead of `kOpt <- dtCvK[accuracy == max(accuracy), k]`.

The plot obtained is as follows:

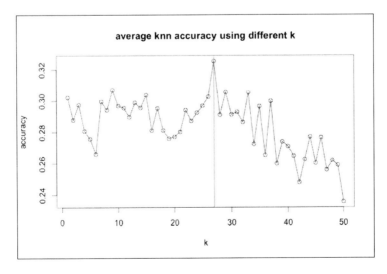

The optimal *k* is 27 and the KNN performs very well if the *k* is in the 22 to 30 range.

In this chapter, we identified *k* performing at its best. However, there are still other parameters that we haven't optimized, such as the distance method. In addition, we can improve the algorithm selecting the features to include and we will explore it in the next section.

# Selecting the data features to include in the model

In the previous section, we set a KNN parameter maximizing the performance. Another tuning option is to define which data we use to build the model. Our table describes the flags using 37 features and we included all of them in the model. However, KNN might perform better including only a subset of them.

The easiest way to select the features is to use a filter (as anticipated in the *Ranking the features using a filter or a dimensionality reduction* section in *Chapter 4, Step 1 – Data Exploration and Feature Engineering*) that estimates the impact of each feature and includes only the most relevant features. After ranking all the features on the basis of their relevance, we can define the n parameters specifying how many of them we include in the model. Then, we can maximize the accuracy depending on n, using an approach similar to the previous section.

The first step is defining how to rank the features. We can use the information gain ratio filter that estimated the impact of each feature ignoring the others. We have already talked about the information gain ratio and its limitations (refer to the *Ranking the features using a filter or a dimensionality reduction* section in *Chapter 4, Step 1 – Data Exploration and Feature Engineering*) and we will use the same R commands, as shown:

```
# rank the features
library('FSelector')
dfGains <- information.gain(
  language~., dtFeatures
  )
dfGains$feature <- row.names(dfGains)
dtGains <- data.table(dfGains)
dtGains <- dtGains[order(attr importance, decreasing = T)]
arrayFeatures <- dtGains[, feature]
```

Here, `arrayFeatures` contains the features sorted by relevance. Now, we can build the model choosing the top *n* features. The options for *n* are the numbers between 1 and the total number of features, and we define `arrayN` containing them, as shown:

```
# define the number of features to test
arrayN <- 1:length(arrayFeatures)
```

In order to store the accuracy of each iteration, we define `dtAccuracyN` as an empty data table and we iteratively add the rows using a `for` loop. The steps are as follows:

1.  Validate KNN using `cvKnn` and store the accuracies in `arrayAccuracy`. We set the *k* parameter equal to `kOpt` (27), that is, the optimal *k* defined in the previous section.

2.  Define the `rowsAccuracyN` data table with the rows to add.

3.  Add the new rows to `dtAccuracyN` using `rbind`.

This is the code generating the `for` loop:

```
for(n in arrayN)
{
  # 1 run the KNN and compute the accuracies
  arrayAccuracy <- cvKnn(
    dtFeatures,
    nIterations = nIterations,
    arrayFeatures = arrayFeatures[1:n],
    k = kOpt
  )

  # 2 define the new data table rows
  rowsAccuracyN <- data.table(
    accuracy = arrayAccuracy,
    n = n
  )

  # 3 add the new rows to the accuracy table
  dtAccuracyN <- rbind(
    dtAccuracyN,
    rowsAccuracyN
  )
}
```

Here, dtAccuracyN contains each iteration accuracy, depending on *n*. We can build a chart containing all the accuracies and their average across different values of *n*, by using the following steps:

1.  Build a chart displaying the accuracy at each iteration:

```
plot(
  x = dtAccuracyN[, n],
  y = dtAccuracyN[, accuracy],
  xlab = 'N', ylab = 'Accuracy',
  main = 'KNN accuracy using different features',
  ylim = c(0, 1),
  col = 'grey'
)
```

2.  Starting from dtAccuracyN, compute the average accuracy for each iteration:

```
dtCvN <- dtAccuracyN[
  , list(accuracy = mean(accuracy)),
  by='n'
  ]
```

3.  Add the points with the average accuracy to the chart:

```
Points(
  x = dtCvN[, n],
  y = dtCvN[, accuracy],
  xlab = 'n', ylab = 'accuracy',
  pch = 16
)
```

The plot obtained is as follows:

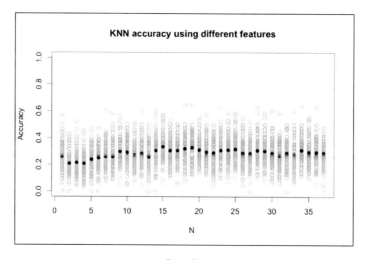

The chart shows that we achieved the best accuracies using high values of *n*. In order to identify the best *n*, we can plot just their averages. Then, we define nOpt that is the *n* performing best and we add a red vertical line corresponding to it, as shown:

```
# plot the average accuracy
plot(
  x = dtCvN[, n],
  y = dtCvN[, accuracy],
  xlab = 'N', ylab = 'Accuracy',
  main = 'Average knn accuracy using different features',
  type = 'o'
)

# identify the n performing best
nOpt <- dtCvN[accuracy == max(accuracy), n]
abline(v = nOpt, col = 'red')
```

The plot obtained is as follows:

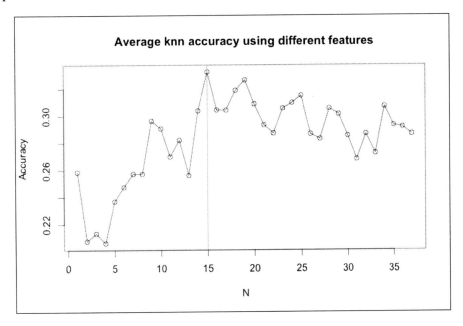

The number of features performing best is **15** and the performance decreases slowly after this point.

In the chart, we can notice that there are some points in which the accuracy decreases a lot adding a new feature (for example, **3, 11, 13**). In these points, we are adding a feature that decreases the performance. What if we just decide not to include it? We can start building the model using the most relevant feature only, and then add the second most relevant feature. If the performance improves, we keep the second feature; otherwise, we discard it. After that, we do the same with the third feature and we repeat this until we have added or discarded each feature. This approach is called wrapper and it allows us to define a better feature set than the filter.

In this section, we identified the best $n$ and the best $k$, so we use them to build KNN with a good performance.

# Tuning features and parameters together

In the previous two sections, we identified the best $k$ using all the features (n=37). Then, using the optimal $k$, we identified the best $n$. What if the algorithm performs better with k=30 and n=25? We haven't explored that combination as well as many other options, so there might be a combination performing better than k=27 and n=15.

In order to identify the best option, the most simple approach is to test all the alternatives. However, if there are too many possible combinations between the variables, we don't have enough computational power to test all of them. In that case, we can identify the optimal parameters using optimization algorithms such as the gradient descend.

Fortunately, in our case, we are tuning only two parameters and we can test just a part of their possible values. For instance, if we choose 20 values of $n$ and 20 values of $k$, we have 400 combinations. In order to do that, we carry out the following steps:

1. Define the options for $k$. Include all features, the KNN had the best performance with k=26 and it performed badly after 40. However, setting a lower $n$, things may change, so we need to test all the possible $k$. In order to limit the number of options, we can limit our testing to the odd numbers. Let's generate all the odd numbers between 1 and 49 using seq. The from and to arguments define the start and end of the sequence. The by argument defines the increment that is 2 to generate the odd numbers. Using seq, we build arrayK containing all the options for $k$, as shown:

```
arrayK <- seq(from = 1, to =  49, by = 2)
```

2. Define the options for *n*. We have already seen that the algorithm performs very badly using just a small feature set, so we can test *n* between 10 and the total number of features, that is, 37. Similar to *k*, we include only the odd numbers:

```
arrayN <- seq(from = 11, to = 37, by = 2)
```

3. Generate all the possible combinations between *k* and *n*. For this purpose, we can use expand.grid. Given two or more vectors, expand.grid generates a data frame with all their possible combinations. In our case, we generate a k column starting from arrayK and a n column starting from arrayN, as shown:

```
dfParameters <- expand.grid(k=arrayK, n=arrayN)
```

4. Convert dfParameters into a data table:

```
dtParameters <- data.table(dfParameters)
```

Now, we can take a look at dtParameters using head:

```
head(dtParameters)
    k  n
1:  1 11
2:  3 11
3:  5 11
4:  7 11
5:  9 11
6: 11 11
```

Here, dtParameters contains a row for each of the 350 combinations. We need to determine the accuracies and store them in a new column called accuracy. In order to do that, we use a for loop running over the rows. The iConfig variable is the row index defined as a number between 1 and the number of rows nrow(dtParameters). There are different combinations, so it might take a while to run this part of the code. After each iteration we build the model using the parameters contained in the row that are:

- **k**: This has the dtParameters[iConfig, k] parameter
- **n**: This has the dtParameters[iConfig, n] parameter

Consider the following code:

```
# validate the knn with different k and nFeatures
for(iConfig in 1:nrow(dtParameters)){

  arrayAccuracy <- cvKnn(
    dtFeatures, nIterations = nIterations,
    arrayFeatures = arrayFeatures[1:dtParameters[iConfig, n]],
    k = dtParameters[iConfig, k]
  )
```

Now, we can compute the `arrayAccuracy` average and add it to `dtParameters`:

```
  # add the average accuracy to dtParameters
  dtParameters[iConfig, accuracy := mean(arrayAccuracy)]
}
```

Each row of `dtParameters` contains a parameter set and its related accuracy. In order to view the accuracies in a more convenient way, we can build a matrix whose rows correspond to n and whose columns correspond to k. Each element of the matrix displays the accuracy. In order to build the matrix, we can use `reshape`, as shown:

```
# reshape dtParameters into a matrix
help(reshape)
```

The `reshape` syntax is quite complex. In our case, that matrix that we want to build is in a `wide` format, so we need to specify `direction = "wide"`. The other arguments define the columns that we use and they are:

- `v.names`: This column defines the matrix values (the accuracies)
- `idvar`: This column defines the matrix rows (the values of n)
- `timevar`: This column defines the matrix columns (the values of k)

Using `reshape`, we can build the `dfAccuracy` data frame, as shown:

```
dfAccuracy <- reshape(
  data = dtParameters,
  direction = "wide",
  v.names = "accuracy",
  idvar = "n",
  timevar = "k"
)
View(dfAccuracy)
```

The n column contains the *n* parameter and we remove it in order to have a data frame with the accuracy only. Then, we convert the data frame into a matrix, as shown:

```
dfAccuracy$n <- NULL
matrixAccuracy <- as.matrix(dfAccuracy)
```

Now, we can specify n and k as the row names and column names respectively, as shown:

```
rownames(matrixAccuracy) <- arrayN
colnames(matrixAccuracy) <- arrayK
View(matrixAccuracy)
```

In order to visualize the accuracy depending on the parameters, we can build a heat map that is a chart representing the matrix. The two chart dimensions are k and n and the color represents the value. We can build this chart using `image`:

```
# plot the performance depending on k and n
help(image)
```

The arguments that we use are:

- z: This is the matrix
- x and y: These are the dimension names, contained in `arrayN` and `arrayK`
- xLab and yLab: These are the axis labels
- col: This is the vector of colors that we display (we can use the `heat.colors` function)

Consider the following code:

```
image(
  x = arrayN, y = arrayK, z = matrixAccuracy,
  xlab = 'n', ylab = 'k',
  col = heat.colors(100)
)
```

The plot obtained is as follows:

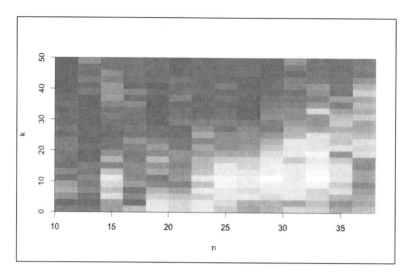

A high accuracy is represented by the pale yellow color and a low accuracy is represented by the red color. We can notice that we achieved the best accuracy with *k* in the 9 to 19 range and *n* in the 29 to 33 range. The worst performance is when *n* is low and *k* is high.

Let's see what the best performing combination is. Consider the following code:

```
# identify the best k-n combination
kOpt <- dtParameters[accuracy == max(accuracy), k]
nOpt <- dtParameters[accuracy == max(accuracy), n]
```

The best combination is `k=11` and `n=33` and we were not able to identify it maximizing the parameters separately. The reason is that the KNN performs well with `k=11` only if we don't include all the features.

In this section, we saw a simple way to optimize two parameters. In other contexts, we need more advanced techniques.

A limit of this approach is that we tuned only two parameters. We can achieve better performances tuning other KNN parameters such as the distance method.

# Summary

In this chapter, we learned how to evaluate the performance of a model as the average accuracy of the prediction. We understood how to determine an accurate cross-validation index expressing the accuracy. Starting from the cross-validation index, we tuned the parameters. In addition, we learned how to select the features using a filter or a frapper and how to tune features and parameters at the same time. This chapter described the last part of building a machine learning solution and the next chapter shows an overview of some of the most important machine learning techniques.

# 7
# Overview of Machine Learning Techniques

There are different machine learning techniques and this chapter gives an overview of the most relevant ones. Some of them have already been introduced in the previous chapters and some are new.

In this chapter, you will learn the following topics:

- The most relevant branches of techniques: supervised and unsupervised learning
- Making predictions with supervised learning
- Identifying hidden patterns and structures with unsupervised learning
- Pros and cons of these techniques

## Overview

There are different categories of machine learning techniques and in this chapter we will see the two most relevant branches — supervised and unsupervised learning, as shown in the following figure:

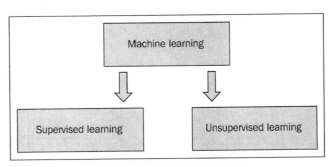

The supervised and unsupervised learning techniques deal with objects described by features. An example of supervised learning techniques is decision tree learning, and an example of unsupervised technique is k-means. In both cases, the algorithms learn from a set of objects and the difference is their target: supervised techniques predict attributes whose nature is already known and unsupervised techniques identify new patterns.

The supervised learning techniques predict an attribute of the objects. The algorithms learn from a training set of objects whose attribute is known and they predict the attribute of other objects. There are two categories of supervised learning techniques: classification and regression. We talk about classification if the predicted attribute is categoric and about regression if the attribute is numeric.

The unsupervised learning techniques identify patterns and structures of a set of objects. The two main branches of unsupervised learning are clustering and dimensionality reduction. The clustering techniques identify homogeneous groups of objects on the basis of their attributes and an example is k-means. Dimensionality reduction techniques identify a small set of significant features describing the objects and an example is the principal component analysis. The difference between clustering and dimensionality reduction depends on the identified attribute that is categoric or numeric respectively, as shown in the following figure:

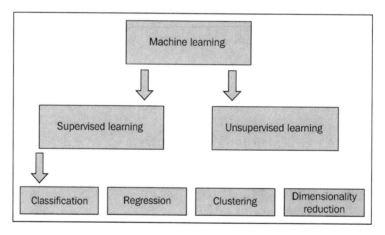

This chapter will show you some popular techniques for each branch. In order to illustrate the techniques, we will reuse the flag dataset of *Chapters 4, Step 1 – Data Exploration and Feature Engineering*; *Chapter 5, Step 2 – Applying Machine Learning Techniques*; and *Chapter 6, Step 3 – Validating the Results* that can be found in the supporting code bundle with this book.

# Supervised learning

This chapter will show you some examples of popular supervised learning algorithms. These techniques are very useful for facing business problems because they make predictions about future attributes and outcomes. In addition, it is possible to measure the accuracy of each technique and/or parameter in order to choose the most suitable one and set it up in the best way.

As anticipated, there are two categories of techniques: classification and regression. However, most of the techniques can be used in both the contexts. Each of the following subsections introduces a different algorithm.

# The k-nearest neighbors algorithm

KNN is a supervised learning algorithm that performs classification or regression. Given a new object, the algorithm predicts its attribute starting from its $k$ neighbors that are its most similar objects. KNN is a lazy learning algorithm in the sense that it directly queries the training data to make a prediction.

In the case of a categoric attribute, the algorithm estimates it as the most common among the similar objects. In the case of a numeric attribute, it computes the median or average between them. In order to state which are the $k$ most *similar* objects, KNN uses a similarity function that evaluates how similar two objects are. In order to measure similarity, the starting point is often a distance matrix expressing the dissimilarity. Then, the algorithm computes the similarity between the new object and each other and picks the $k$ most similar objects.

In our example, we will use the flag dataset and the features are the number of stripes and the number of colors in the flags. The attribute that we want to predict starting from its flag attributes is the language of a new country.

The training set is composed of some countries in such a way that there are no two countries with the same flag features. First, let's visualize the data. We can show the countries in a chart whose dimensions are the two features and whose color is the language, as follows:

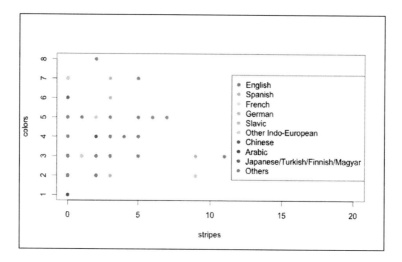

We have two new countries with:

- 7 stripes and 4 colors
- 3 stripes and 7 colors

We want to determine the language of two new countries using a 4-nearest-neighbor algorithm. We can add the two countries to the chart and determine the 4 closest points for each of them, as shown here:

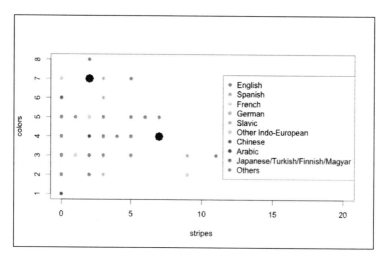

With regard to the country on the right-hand side of the chart, all its 4 closest neighbors belong to **Others**, so we estimate that its language is **Others**. The other country has a mixed neighborhood: 1 English, 1 Other Indo-European, and 2 Spanish countries. The most common language is Spanish, so we estimate that it is a Spanish-speaking country.

The KNN is a simple and scalable algorithm that achieves good results in many contexts. However, in the presence of many features, the similarity function takes account of all of them, including the less relevant, making it difficult to use the distance. In that context, the KNN is not able to identify the meaningful nearest neighbors and this issue is called the curse of dimensionality. A solution is to reduce the dimensionality by selecting the most relevant features or using a dimensionality reduction technique (this is the topic of the next section).

# Decision tree learning

Decision tree learning is a supervised learning algorithm that builds a classification or regression tree. Each leaf of the tree represents the attribute estimation and each node splits the data accordingly with a condition of the features.

The decision tree learning is an eager method in the sense that it uses a training set to build a model that doesn't require you to query the data. All the other supervised learning techniques are eager as well.

The target of the algorithm is to define the most relevant feature and split the set in two groups accordingly with it. Then, for each group, the algorithm identifies its most relevant feature and divides the objects of the groups into two parts. This procedure goes on until we identify the leaves as small groups of objects. For each leaf, the algorithm estimates the feature as a mode, if it is categoric, or average, if it is numeric. After building the tree, if we have too many leaves, we can define a level in which we stop splitting the tree. In this way, each leaf will contain a reasonably big group. This procedure of stopping splitting is called pruning. In this way, we find a less complex and more accurate prediction.

In our example, we want to determine the language of a new country starting from different flag attributes, such as colors and patterns. The algorithm builds the tree learning from a training set. Let's visualize it:

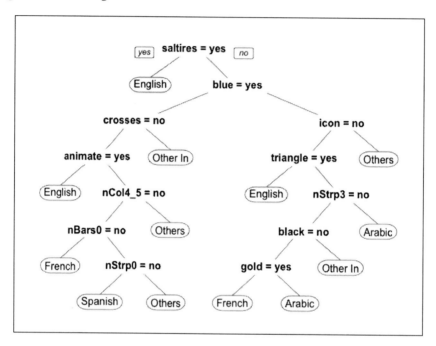

In any node, if the answer is **true**, we go to the left, and if the answer is **false**, we go to the right. First, the model identifies the most relevant attribute that is **saltires**. If a flag contains a saltire, we go to the left and we determine that the related country is English. Otherwise, we go to the right and we check if the flag contains the blue color. Then, we go on checking the conditions until we reach a leaf.

Let's suppose that we built the tree without taking account of the Spanish flag. How do we estimate the language of Spain? Starting from the top, we check the conditions on each node we encounter.

These are the steps:

1. The flag doesn't contain a saltire, so we go to the left.

2. The flag contains the blue color, so we go to the right.

3. The flag doesn't contain a cross, so `crosses = no` is `true` and we go to the left.

4. The flag doesn't contain an animated image, so we go to the right.

5. The flag has two main colors, so number of colors not equal to 4 or 5 is true and we go to the left.

6. The flag doesn't contain any bars, so we go to the left.

The flag doesn't have any vertical stripes, so nStrp0 = no is true and we go to the left, as shown here:

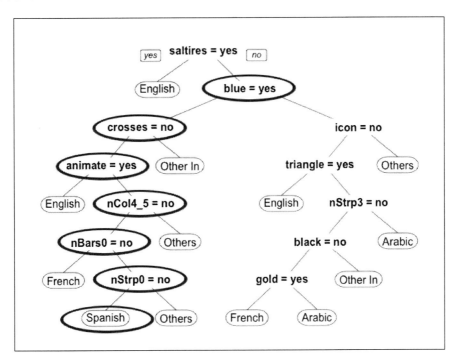

In the end, the estimated language is Spanish.

The decision tree learning can deal with numeric and/or categoric features and attributes, so it can be applied in different contexts with just a little data preparation. In addition, it is applicable when there are many features, different from other algorithms. A disadvantage is that the algorithm can overfit in the sense that the model is too close to the data and is more complicated than the reality, although pruning can help with this.

# Linear regression

Linear regression is a statistical model identifying a relationship between numeric variables. Given a set of objects described by the $y$ attribute and the x1, ..., and xn features, the model defines a relationship between the features and the attribute. The relationship is described by the linear function $y = a0 + a1 * x1 + ... + an * xn$, and a0, ..., and an are parameters defined by the method in such a way that the relationship is as close as possible to the data.

In the case of machine learning, linear regression can be used to predict a numeric attribute. The algorithm learns from the training dataset to determine the parameters. Then, given a new object, the model inserts its features into the linear function to estimate the attribute.

In our example, we want to estimate the population of a country starting from its area. First, let's visualize the data about the area (in thousand km²) and the population (in millions), as shown in the following figure:

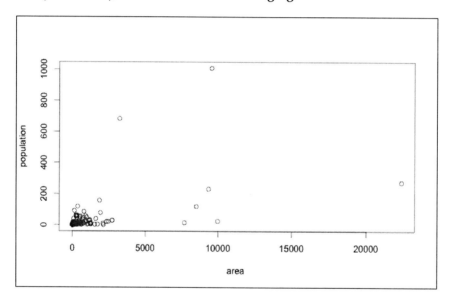

Most of the countries have an area below 3000 thousand km2 and a population below 200 million and just a few countries have a much higher area and/or population. For this reason, most of the points are concentrated in the bottom-left area of the chart. In order to spread the points, we can transform the features using the logarithmic area and population, as shown in the following figure:

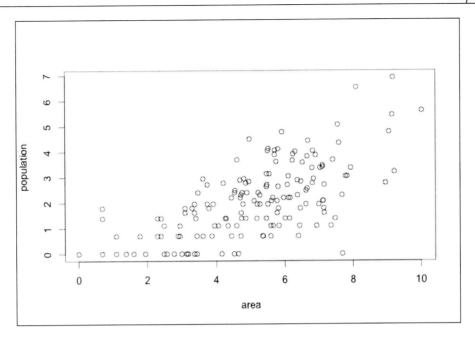

The target of linear regression is to identify a linear relationship that is as close to the data as possible. In our case, we have two dimensions, so we can visualize the relationship using a line. Given the area, the linear regression estimates that the population is on the line. Let's see it in the chart with the logarithmic features:

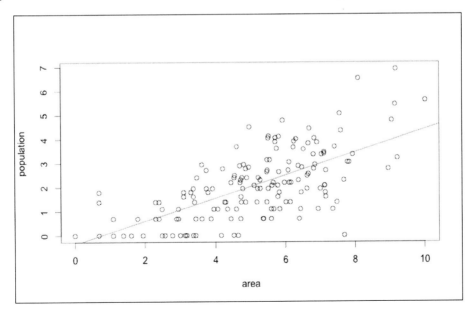

Given a new country about which we know the area, we can estimate its population using the regression line. In the chart, there is a new country of which we know the area. The linear regression estimates that its point is on the red line.

Linear regression is a very simple and basic technique. The disadvantage is that it requires numeric features and attributes, so there are many contexts in which it is not applicable. However, it is possible to convert the categoric features into a numeric format using dummy variables or other techniques.

Another disadvantage is that the model makes strong assumptions on how the features and the attributes are related. The function estimating the output is linear, so in some contexts it might be far from the real relationship. In addition, if in reality the features interact with each other, the model is not able to keep track of the interaction. It's possible to solve this problem using a transformation that makes the relationship linear. It is also possible to define new features expressing non-linear interactions.

The linear regression is very basic and it is the starting point of some other techniques. For instance, the logistic regression predicts an attribute whose value is in the 0 to 1 range.

# Perceptron

**Artificial Neural Networks (ANN)** are the supervised learning techniques whose logic is similar to biological neural systems. A simple ANN technique is the single-layer perceptron and it is a classification technique estimating a binary attribute whose value can be 0 or 1. The perceptron works like a neuron in the sense that it sums the impact of all the inputs and outputs to 1 if the sum is above a defined threshold. The model is based on the following parameters:

- A weight for each feature, defining its impact
- A threshold above which the estimated output is 1

Starting from the features, the model estimates the attribute through these steps

- Compute the output through a linear regression: multiply each feature by its weight and sum all of them
- Estimate the attribute to 1 if the output is above the threshold and to 0 otherwise

The models are as shown in the following figure:

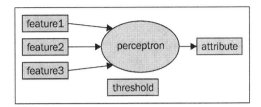

In the beginning, the algorithm builds the perceptron with a defined set of coefficients and with a threshold. Then, the algorithm iteratively improves the coefficients using the training set. At each step, the algorithm estimates the attribute of each object. Then, the algorithm computes the difference between the real and the estimated attribute and uses the difference to modify the coefficients. In many situations, the algorithm does not reach a stable set of coefficients that are not modified, so we need to define at which point we stop. In the end, we have a perception defined by a set of coefficients and we can use it to estimate the attribute of new objects.

The perceptron is a simple example of a neural network and it allows us to easily understand the impact of the variables. However, the perceptron depends on a linear regression, so it is limited in the same way: the feature impact is linear and the features can't interact with each other.

# Ensembles

Each algorithm has some weaknesses leading to incorrect results. What if we were able to solve the same problem using different algorithms and to pick the best result? If just a few algorithms commit the same mistake, we can just ignore them. It is not possible to determine which result is correct and which is not, but there is another option. By performing supervised learning on a new object, we can apply different algorithms and pick the most common or average result among them. In this way, if most of the algorithms identify the correct estimation, we will take it into account. The ensemble methods are based on this principle: they combine different classification or regression algorithms to increase their accuracy.

An ensemble method requires variability between the results coming from different algorithms and/or training datasets. Some options are:

- **Changing the algorithm configuration**: The algorithm is the same and its parameters vary within a range.

- **Changing the algorithm**: We predict the attribute using different techniques. In addition, for each technique, we can use different configurations.

- **Using different data subsets**: The algorithm is the same and every time it learns from a different random subset of the training data.

- **Using different data samples (bagging)**: The algorithm is the same and it learns from a bootstrap sample, that is, a set of objects picked randomly from the training dataset. The same object can be picked more than once.

The final result combines the output of all the algorithms. In the case of classification, we use the mode, and in the case of regression, we use the average or median.

We can build an ensemble algorithm using any combination of supervised learning techniques, so there are several options. An example is a random forest that combines decision tree learning algorithms using bagging (the technique explained in the last bullet point in the previous list).

The ensemble methods often perform much better than the single algorithms. In the case of classification, the ensemble removes the biases affecting just a small part of the algorithms. However, the logic of different algorithms is often related and the same bias might be common. In this case, the ensemble keeps the bias.

The ensemble methods don't always work in the case of regression problems since the biases affect the final result. For instance, if there is just an algorithm computing a very biased result, the average will be highly affected by that. In this context, the median works better since it is much more stable and it is not affected by outliers.

# Unsupervised learning

This chapter shows some unsupervised learning techniques. When facing a business problem, these techniques allow us to identify hidden structures and patterns and perform exploratory data analysis. In addition, unsupervised learning can simplify the problem, allowing us to build more accurate and less elaborated solutions. These techniques can also be used in the solution of the problem itself.

The two branches of techniques are clustering and dimensionality reduction and most of them are not applicable in both the contexts. This chapter shows some popular techniques.

# k-means

k-means is a centroid-based clustering technique. Given a set of objects, the algorithm identifies $k$ homogeneous clusters. k-means is centroid-based in the sense that each cluster is defined by its centroid representing its average object.

The target of the algorithm is to identify $k$ centroids. Then, the k-means associates each object to the closest centroid, defining $k$ clusters. The algorithm starts with a random set of centroids and it iteratively changes them, improving the clustering.

In our example, the data is about the country flags and the two features are the number of stripes and the number of colors. We select a subset of the countries in such a way that there are no two flags with the same value of the attributes. Our target is to identify two homogeneous groups of countries. The first step of the k-means is identifying two random centroids. Let's visualize the data and the centroids in a chart:

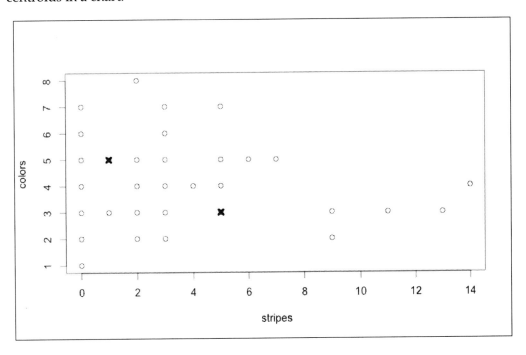

The **o** represents the country flags and the **x** represents the centroids. Before running k-means, we need to define a distance that is a way of determining dissimilarity between objects. For instance, in the preceding chart, we can use the Euclidean distance that expresses the length of the line connecting two points. The algorithm is iterative and each step consists of the following steps:

1. For each point, determine the centroid whose distance is the minimum. Then, assign the point to the cluster related to the closest centroid.

2. Recompute the centroid of each cluster in such a way that it is the average between its objects.

In the end, we have two clusters with the related centroids representing average objects. Let's visualize them, as shown here:

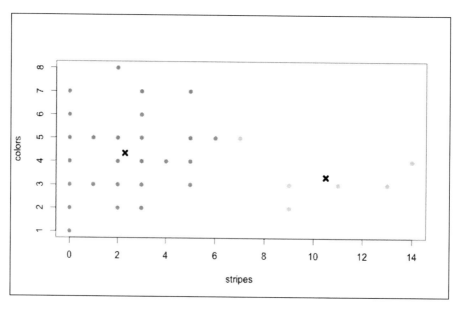

The colors represent the clusters and the black **x** represents the final centroids.

k-means is one of the most popular clustering techniques because it is easy to understand and it doesn't require a lot of computational power. However, the algorithm has some limitations. It contains a random component, so if we run it twice on the same set of data it will probably identify different clusters. Another disadvantage is that it is not able to identify the clusters in some specific contexts, for instance, when the clusters have different sizes or elaborated shapes. k-means is a very simple and basic algorithm and it is the starting point to some more elaborate techniques.

# Hierarchical clustering

Hierarchical clustering is a branch of clustering techniques. Starting from a set of objects, the target builds a hierarchy of clusters. In agglomerative hierarchical clustering, each object belongs to a different cluster in the beginning. Then, the algorithm merges the clusters until there is one cluster containing all the objects. After having identified the hierarchy, we can define the clusters and stop their merging at any point.

During each agglomeration step, the algorithm merges the two most similar clusters and there are some parameters defining the similarity. First, we need to define a way to measure how similar two objects are. There are several options, depending on the situation. Then, we need to define the similarity between clusters; the methods are called **linkage**. In order to measure the similarity, we start defining a distance function that is the opposite. To determine the distance between cluster1 and cluster2, we measure the distance between every possible object of cluster1 and every object of cluster2. Some options to measure the distance between the two clusters are:

- **Single linkage**: This is the minimum distance
- **Complete linkage**: This is the maximum distance
- **Average linkage**: This is the average distance

Depending on the linkage, the results of the algorithms will be different.

The example uses the same data as k-means. The country flags are represented by the number of stripes and colors and we want to identify homogeneous groups. The distance that we use is the Euclidean (just the distance between two points) and the linkage is complete. First, let's identify the clusters from their hierarchy, as shown in the following figure:

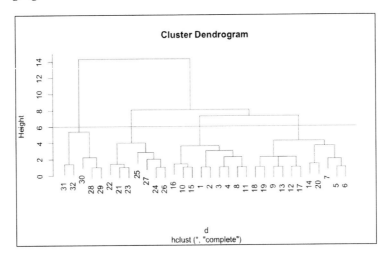

The chart is called a **dendrogram** and at the bottom of the chart every object belongs to a different cluster. Then, going up, we merge the clusters until all the objects belong to the same cluster. The height is the distance at which the algorithm merges the clusters. For instance, at a height of 3, all the clusters whose distance is below 3 are already merged.

The red line is at a height of 6 and it defines when we stop merging and below it the objects are divided in 4 clusters. Now we can visualize the clusters in a chart as follows:

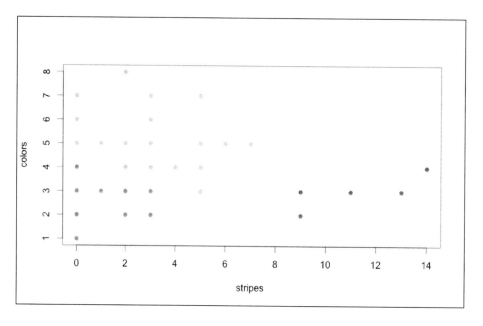

The colors of the points represent the clusters. The algorithm has correctly identified the group on the right and has split the group on the left in three parts in a good way.

There are different options for the hierarchic cluster and some of them produce very good results in some contexts. Different from the k-means, the algorithm is deterministic, so it always leads to the same result.

A big disadvantage of hierarchic cluster is the computational time (O(n3)) that makes it impossible to apply it on large datasets. Another lack is the manual component to choose the algorithm configuration and the dendrogram cut. In order to identify a good solution, we usually need to run the algorithm with different configurations and to visualize the dendrogram to define its cut.

# PCA

**Principal Components Analysis (PCA)** is a statistical procedure transforming the
features. The PCA logic is based on the concepts of linear correlation and variance.
In a machine learning context, the PCA is a dimensionality reduction technique.

Starting with the features describing a set of objects, the target defines other variables
that are linearly uncorrelated with each other. The output is a new set of variables
defined as linear combinations of the initial features. In addition, the new variables
are ranked on the basis of their relevance. The number of the new variables is less
than or equal to the initial number of features and it is possible to select the most
relevant features. Then, we are able to define a smaller set of features, reducing the
problem dimension.

The algorithm starts defining the feature combination with the highest variance.
Then, at each step, it iteratively defines another feature combination maximizing the
variance, under the condition that the new combination is not linearly correlated
with the others.

In the example of *Chapter 4, Step 1 – Data Exploration and Feature Engineering, Chapter
5, Step 2 – Applying Machine Learning Techniques*, and *Chapter 6, Step 3 – Validating the
Results*, we have defined 37 attributes describing each country flag. Applying the PCA,
we can define 37 new attributes defined as linear combination of the variables. The
attributes are ranked by relevance, so we can select the top six and in this way have a
small table describing the flag. In this way, we are able to build a supervised learning
model estimating the language on the basis of six relevant features.

In the presence of a lot of features, the PCA allows us to define a smaller set of
relevant variables. However, this technique is not applicable in all the contexts. A
lack is that the result depends on how the features are scaled, so it is necessary to
standardize the variables first.

Dealing with a supervised learning problem, we can use the PCA to reduce its
dimensionality. However, the PCA only takes into account the features, ignoring
how they are related with the attribute to predict, so it might select feature
combinations that are not very relevant to the problem.

# Summary

In this chapter, we learned about the main branches of machine learning techniques: supervised and unsupervised learning. We saw how to estimate a numeric or categoric attribute using supervised learning techniques such as KNN, decision tree, linear regression, and neural networks. We saw that it is possible to increase performance using ensembles that are techniques combining different supervised learning algorithms. We learned how to identify homogeneous groups using clustering techniques such as k-means and hierarchic clustering. We have also understood the importance of dimensionality reduction techniques such as the PCA to transform the features defining a smaller set of variables.

The next chapter shows an example of a business problem that can be faced using machine learning techniques. We will also see examples of both supervised and unsupervised learning techniques.

# 8
# Machine Learning Examples Applicable to Businesses

The purpose of this chapter is to show you how machine learning helps in solving a business problem. Most of the techniques have already been explored in the previous chapter, so the pace of this chapter is fast. The techniques are about unsupervised and supervised learning. Unsupervised algorithms extract hidden structures from data and supervised techniques forecast an attribute. This chapter solves a business challenge using techniques belonging to the two branches.

In this chapter, you will learn how to:

- Apply the machine learning approach to a business problem
- Segment the customer base of a bank
- Identify the target of a marketing campaign
- Choose the technique performing better

## Overview of the problem

A Portuguese banking institution launches a phone call marketing campaign. The institution has limited resources, so it needs to choose the target clients. Starting from the data about a past campaign, we can give some support to the company using machine learning techniques. The data shows personal details of the clients and information about previous marketing campaigns. The target of machine learning algorithms is to identify the clients that are more likely to subscribe. Starting from the data, the algorithms need to understand how to use new clients' data to predict how likely each of them will subscribe.

# Data overview

The data consists of approximately more than 2,500 clients affected by a marketing campaign consisting of one or more phone calls. We have some details about the clients and we know who subscribed.

Each row of the table corresponds to a client and there is a column displaying the output that is yes if the client subscribed and no otherwise. The other columns are features describing the clients and they are:

- **Personal details**: This incudes details such as age, job, marital status, education, credit default, average yearly balance, housing, and personal loan
- **Communication with the company**: This incudes details such as contact type, last contact month and weekday, last call duration, and number of contacts
- **Previous campaigns**: This incudes details such as number of days before the previous campaign, number of past contacts, and past outcomes

This is a sample of the table. The y column displays the attribute to predict yes if the client subscribed and no otherwise.

| Age | Job | Marital status | ... | Contact | ... | y |
|---|---|---|---|---|---|---|
| 30 | services | married | | cellular | | no |
| 33 | management | single | | telephone | | yes |
| 41 | blue-collar | single | | unknown | | no |
| 35 | self-employed | married | | telephone | | no |

The data is stored in bank.csv and we can load them into R building a data table. The sep=';' field specifies that the fields in the file are separated by a semicolon, as follows:

```
library(data.table)
dtBank <- data.table(read.csv('bank.csv', sep=';'))
```

The duration feature displays the number of seconds in the final call. The target of our analysis is to define which clients to call and we cannot know the duration before contacting the client. In addition, after knowing a call duration, we already know whether the client has subscribed or not, so it is pointless to use this attribute to predict the outcome. For these reasons, we removed the duration feature, as follows:

```
# remove the duration
dtBank[, duration := NULL]
```

The next step is to explore the data in order to understand the context.

# Exploring the output

In this subsection, we quickly explore and transform the data.

The `y` output is categoric and the possible outcomes are `yes` and `no` and our target is to visualize the proportions. For this purpose, we can build a pie chart using these steps:

1. Count how many clients subscribed and how many didn't using `table`:

   ```
   dtBank[, table(y)]
   y
      no   yes
    4000   521
   ```

2. Determine the percentage of clients subscribing and not subscribing:

   ```
   dtBank[, table(y) / .N]
   y
         no       yes
    0.88476  0.11524
   ```

3. Build a function determining the percentages starting from the proportions:

   ```
   DefPercentage <- function(frequency)
   {
     percentage = frequency / sum(frequency)
     percentage = round(percentage * 100)
     percentage = paste(percentage, '%')
     return(percentage)
   }
   ```

4. Determine the percentages:

   ```
   defPercentage(dtBank[, table(y) / .N])
   [1] "88 %" "12 %"
   ```

5. Look at the help of `barplot` that is the R function building bar charts:

   ```
   help(barplot)
   ```

6. Define the barplot input:

   ```
   tableOutput <- dtBank[, table(y)]
   colPlot <- rainbow(length(tableOutput))
   percOutput <- defPercentage(tableOutput)
   ```

7. Build the barplot:

```
barplot(
    height = tableOutput,
    names.arg = percOutput,
    col = colPlot,
    legend.text = names(tableOutput),
    xlab = 'Subscribing'
    ylab = 'Number of clients',
    main = 'Proportion of clients subscribing'
)
```

The plot obtained is as follows:

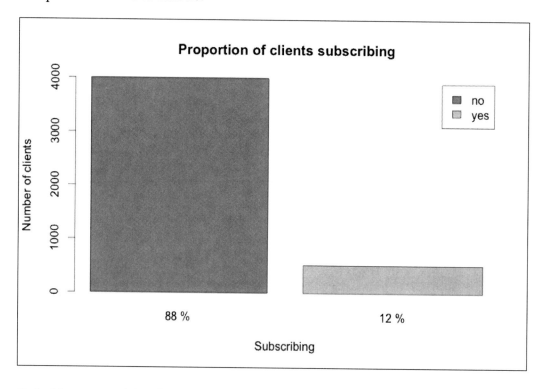

Only 12 percent of the clients subscribed, so the output values are not equally distributed. The next step is to explore all the data.

# Exploring and transforming features

Similar to the output, we can build some charts to explore the features. Let's first take a look at them using `str`:

```
str(dtBank)
Classes 'data.table' and 'data.frame':    4521 obs. of  16 variables:
 $ age      : int  30 33 35 30 59 35 36 39 41 43 ...
 $ job      : Factor w/ 12 levels "admin.","blue-collar",..: 11 8 5 5
2 5 7 10 3 8 ...
 $ marital  : Factor w/ 3 levels "divorced","married",..: 2 2 3 2 2 3
2 2 2 2 ...
 ...
```

The features belong to two data types:

- **Categoric**: This data type stores features in the factor format
- **Numeric**: This data type stores features in the integer format

The charts for the categoric features are different from the numeric ones, so we need to split the features in two groups. We can define a vector containing the categoric features and another vector for the numeric features by using the following steps:

1. Define each column class using `lapply`:

   ```
   classFeatures <- lapply(dtBank, class)
   ```

2. Remove the `y` column containing the output:

   ```
   classFeatures <- classFeatures[names(classFeatures) != 'y']
   ```

3. Determine the categoric features:

   ```
   featCategoric <- names(classFeatures)[
     classFeatures == 'factor'
     ]
   ```

4. Determine the numeric features:

   ```
   featNumeric <- names(classFeatures)[
     classFeatures == 'integer'
     ]
   ```

Similar to the output, we can build a pie chart for each of the nine categoric features. In order to avoid having too many charts, we can put three pies in the same chart. The R function is `par` and it allows a grid of charts to be defined:

```
help(par)
```

The input that we need is:

- `mfcol`: This is a vector containing the number of columns and rows. For each feature, we build a chart with the pie and one with its legend. We put the pie charts on the bottom row and the legends on the top. Then, we have two rows and three columns.

- `mar`: This is a vector defining the plot margins:

  ```
  par(mfcol = c(2, 3), mar = c(3, 4, 1, 2))
  ```

Now, we can build the histograms using a `for` loop:

```
for(feature in featCategoric){
```

Perform the following steps inside the `for` loop:

1. Define the pie chart input:

   ```
   TableFeature <- dtBank[, table(get(feature))]
   rainbCol <- rainbow(length(tableFeature))
   percFeature <- defPercentage(tableFeature)
   ```

2. Define a new plot with the legend consisting of the feature names matched with their color. We add the feature name as the legend title:

   ```
   plot.new()
   legend(
     'top', names(tableFeature),
     col = rainbCol, pch = 16,
     title = feature
   )
   ```

3. Build the histogram that will be displayed on the bottom row:

   ```
   barplot(
     height = tableFeature,
     names.arg = percFeature,
     col = colPlot,
     xlab = feature,
     ylab = 'Number of clients'
   )
   }
   ```

We built three charts containing three categoric features each. Let's take a look at the first one:

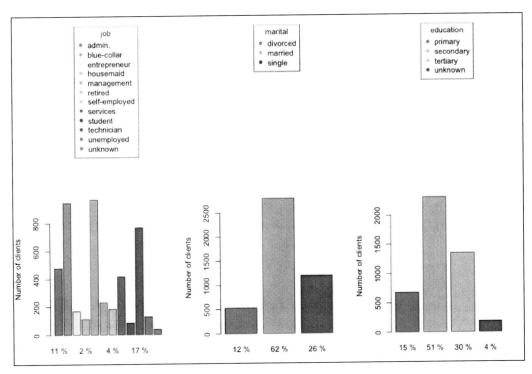

The `job` attribute has different levels and some of them have a significant number of clients. Then, we can define a dummy variable for each relevant job and ignore the others. In order to identify the most relevant jobs, we determine the percentage of people belonging to each level. Then, we set a threshold and ignore all levels whose percentage is below the threshold. In this case, the threshold is 0.08, that is, 8 percent. After defining the new dummy columns, we remove `job`:

```
percJob <- dtBank[, table(job) / .N]
colRelevant <- names(percJob)[percJob > 0.08]
for(nameCol in colRelevant){
  newCol <- paste('job', nameCol, sep='_')
  dtBank[, eval(newCol) := ifelse(job == nameCol, 1, 0)]
}
dtBank[, job := NULL]
```

Here, `marital`, defining the marital status, has three levels out of which `divorced` and `single` have a smaller, although significant, slice. We can define two dummy variables defining the three levels:

```
dtBank[, single := ifelse(marital == 'single', 1, 0)]
dtBank[, divorced := ifelse(marital == 'divorced', 1, 0)]
dtBank[, marital := NULL]
```

With regard to `education`, more than half of the clients received a secondary education, so we can assume that the 4 percent of `unknown` are `secondary`. Then, we have three attributes and we can define two dummy variables:

```
dtBank[, edu_primary := ifelse(education == 'primary', 1, 0)]
dtBank[, edu_tertiary := ifelse(education == 'tertiary', 1, 0)]
dtBank[, education := NULL]
```

The plot obtained is as follows:

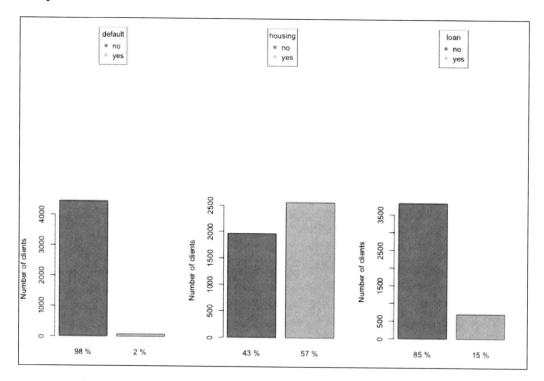

The **default**, **housing**, and **loan** attributes have two different levels, so they can be converted into numerical form using `as.numeric`. In order to have `0` if the attribute was `no` and `1` if the attribute was `yes`, we subtract 1, as follows:

```
dtBank[, housing := as.numeric(housing) - 1]
dtBank[, default := as.numeric(default) - 1]
dtBank[, loan := as.numeric(loan) - 1]
```

The histogram obtained is as follows:

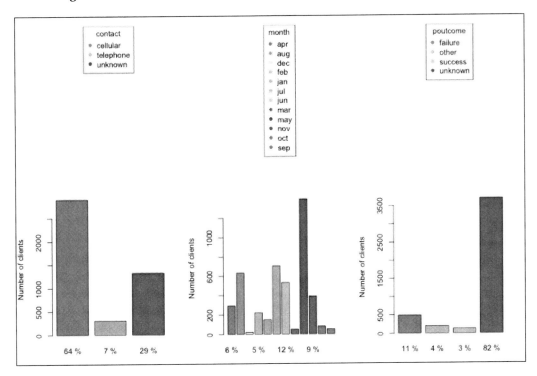

Here, **contact** has three options out of which one is **unknown**. All the options have a significant slice, so we can define two dummy variables, as follows:

```
dtBank[, cellular := ifelse(contact == 'cellular', 1, 0)]
dtBank[, telephone := ifelse(contact == 'telephone', 1, 0)]
dtBank[, contact := NULL]
```

We can convert `month` into a numeric variable in which January corresponds to 1 and December to 12. The feature values are the month names abbreviated without a capital letter, for example, `jan` for `January`. In order to define the numeric feature, we define a vector whose first element is `jan`, second element is `feb`, and so on. Then, using `which`, we can identify the corresponding element of the vector. For instance, `apr` is the fourth element of the vector, so using `which` we obtain 4. In order to build the vector with the ordered month names, we use `month.abb` containing the abbreviated month names and `tolower` to uncapitalize the first letter, as follows:

```
Months <- tolower(month.abb)
months <- c(
    'jan', 'feb', 'mar', 'apr', 'may', 'jun',
    'jul', 'aug', 'sep', 'oct', 'nov', 'dec'
)
dtBank[
  , month := which(month == months),
  by=1:nrow(dtBank)
  ]
```

In `poutcome`, `success` and `failure` have a small portion of the clients. However, they are very relevant, so we define two dummy variables:

```
dtBank[, past_success := ifelse(poutcome == 'success', 1, 0)]
dtBank[, past_failure := ifelse(poutcome == 'failure', 1, 0)]
dtBank[, poutcome := NULL]
```

We converted all the categoric features into the numeric format. The next step is to explore the numeric features and transform them if necessary.

There are six numeric features and we can build a plot about each of them. The chart is a histogram showing how the values of the feature are distributed. In order to visualize all the figures in the same charts, we can put them in a 3 x 2 grid using `par`. The arguments are as follows:

- `mfrow`: Similar to `mfcol`, it defines a grid of figures. The difference is just the order in which we add the figures to the grid.
- `mar`: We set the margins to their default, that is, `c(5, 4, 4, 2) + 0.1`, as follows:

```
par(mfrow=c(3, 2), mar=c(5, 4, 4, 2) + 0.1)
```

We can build the histograms using `hist`. The input is as follows:

- `x`: This is the vector with the data
- `main`: This is the plot title
- `xlab`: This is the label under the x-axis

We can use `hist` directly inside the data table square brackets. In order to build all the charts in one step, we use a `for` loop:

```
for(feature in featNumeric){
    dtBank[, hist(x = get(feature), main=feature, xlab = feature)]
}
```

The histogram obtained is as follows:

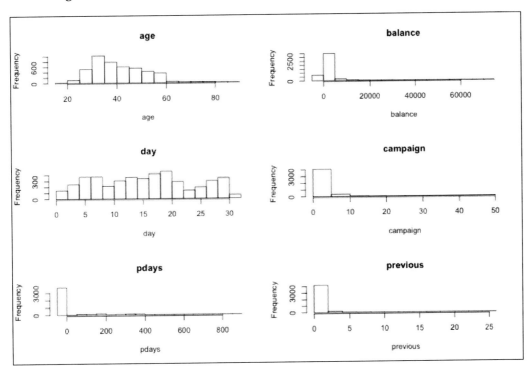

Here, **age** and **day** are evenly distributed across their possible values, so they don't require any treatment. The remaining features are concentrated in the small values, so we need to transform them. The function that we use to define the transformed feature is the logarithm and it allows us to have more spreaded values. The logarithm works on features having values greater than 0, so we need to remove the negative values from the feature.

In order to avoid zeros, add 1 to the feature before computing the logarithm.

Accordingly with the data description, pdays is equal to -1 if the institution has not contacted the client before. In order to identify the clients contacted for the first time, we can define a new dummy variable that is 1 if pdays is equal to -1. Then, we replace all the negative values with 0, as follows:

```
dtBank[, not_contacted := ifelse(pdays == -1, 1, 0)]
dtBank[pdays == -1, pdays := 0]
```

The balance feature represents the past balance and we can define a dummy variable that is 1, if the balance is negative. Then, we replace the negative balances with 0:

```
dtBank[, balance_negative := ifelse(balance < 0, 1, 0)]
dtBank[balance < 0, balance := 0]
```

Now, we can compute the logarithm to all the features. Since the input of a logarithm must be positive and some features are equal to 0, we add 1 to each feature before computing the logarithm:

```
dtBank[, pdays := log(pdays + 1)]
dtBank[, balance := log(balance + 1)]
dtBank[, campaign := log(campaign + 1)]
dtBank[, previous := log(previous + 1)]
```

We have converted all the features into the numeric format. Now, we can take a look at the new features table:

```
str(dtBank)
View(dtBank)
```

The only column that is not numeric or integer is the output y. We can convert it into the numeric format and change its name to output:

```
dtBank[, output := as.numeric(y) - 1]
dtBank[, y := NULL]
```

We loaded and cleaned the data. Now we are ready to build the machine learning models.

# Clustering the clients

In order to address the next marketing campaign, we need to identify the clients that are more likely to subscribe. Since it's hard to evaluate the clients one by one, we can determine homogeneous groups of clients and identify the most promising groups.

Starting from the past data, we cluster the clients on the basis of their personal details. Then, given a new client, we identify the most similar group and associate the new client to it. We don't have information about the customer behavior of the new clients, so clustering is based on the personal attributes only.

There are different techniques performing clustering and in this section we use a relevant algorithm that is hierarchical clustering. A parameter of hierarchical clustering is linkage, which is the way of computing the distance between two groups. The main options are:

- **Single linkage**: This is the minimum distance between an object of the first group and an object of the second group
- **Complete linkage**: This is the maximum distance between an object of the first group and an object of the second group
- **Average linkage**: This is the average distance between an object of the first group and an object of the second group

In our case, we choose the average linkage and this choice comes from testing the three options.

We define dtPers containing the personal features only, as follows:

```
featPers <- c(
  'age', 'default', 'balance', 'balance_negative',
  'housing', 'loan',
  'job_admin.', 'job_blue-collar',  'job_management',
  'job_services', 'job_technician',
  'single', 'divorced', 'edu_primary', 'edu_tertiary'
)
dtPers <- dtBank[, featPers, with=F]
```

Now, we can apply hierarchical clustering and the steps are as follows:

1. Define the dissimilarity matrix:
   ```
   d <- dist(dtPers, method = 'euclidean')
   ```

2. Build the hierarchical clustering model:
   ```
   hcOut <- hclust(d, method = 'average')
   ```

3.  Visualize the dendrogram. The `par` method defines the plot layout that in this case contains just one chart and `plot` contains an argument improving the appearance. The `labels` and `hang` features avoid having a messy chart in the bottom and the other arguments specify the plot title and the axis labels, as shown:

```
par(mfrow = c(1, 1))
plot(
  hcOut,
  labels = FALSE,
  hang = -1,
  main = 'Dendrogram',
  xlab = 'Client clusters',
  ylab = 'Agglomeration distance'
)
```

The histogram obtained is as follows:

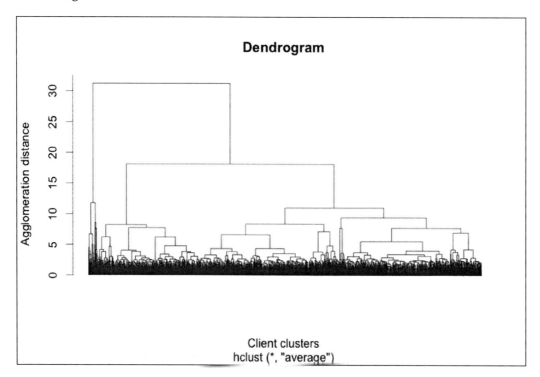

We can identify three clusters cutting the dendrogram around the height of **40**. There is also another option that is cutting the dendrogram at a lower level (around 18), identifying seven clusters. We can explore both the options and visualize the two splits on the dendrogram using `rect.hclust`, as follows:

```
k1 <- 3
k2 <- 7
par(mfrow=c(1, 1))
rect.hclust(hcOut, k = k1)
rect.hclust(hcOut, k = k2)
```

The histogram obtained is as follows:

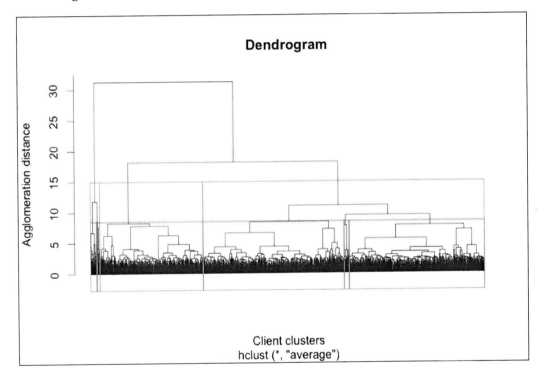

In order to identify the most successful cluster, we can display the proportion of clients that subscribed using a pie chart putting as its title the number of clients in the cluster. Let's see the chart for the three clusters of the first split. The steps to build the pie charts are similar to the steps we performed earlier:

1. Define a data table containing the output attribute:

```
dtClust <- dtBank[, 'output', with = F]
```

2. Add two columns defining clusters to the data table. Each column corresponds to a different number of clusters:

```
dtClust[, clusterHc1 := cutree(hclOut, k = k1)]
dtClust[, clusterHc2 := cutree(hclOut, k = k2)]
```

3. Define the plot layout with one row and three columns. The oma argument defines the outer margins:

```
par(mfrow = c(1, 3), oma = c(0, 0, 10, 0))
```

4. Using commands similar to the data exploration, build three histograms showing the percentage of clients subscribing or not to each cluster:

```
for(iCluster in 1:k1){
  tableClust <- dtClust[
    clusterHc1 == iCluster,
    table(output)
  ]
  sizeCluster <- dtClust[, sum(clusterHc1 == iCluster)]
  titlePie <- paste(sizeCluster, 'clients')
  barplot(
    height = tableClust,
    names.arg = defPercentage(tableClust),
    legend.text = c('no', 'yes'),
    col = c('blue', 'red'),
    main = titlePie
  )
}
```

5. Add the title of the charts:

```
mtext(
  text = 'Hierarchic clustering, n = 3',
  outer = TRUE, line = 1, cex = 2
)
```

The histogram obtained is as follows:

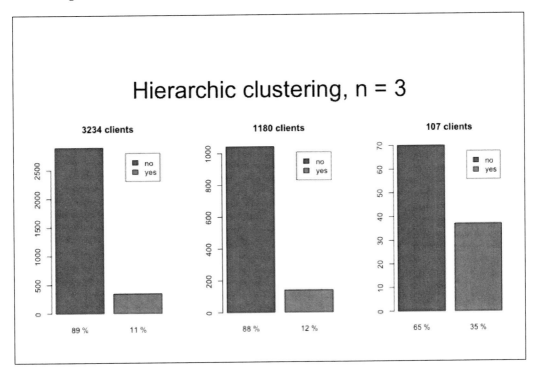

The first and second clusters contain the majority of clients and the campaign hasn't been particularly successful on them. The third cluster is smaller and a significantly higher percentage of its clients subscribed. Then, we can start the marketing campaign targeting new clients similar to the third cluster.

Using the same R commands, we can visualize the same charts for the seven clusters identified by the second split, as follows:

1. Define the plot layout with two rows and four columns:

```
par(mfrow = c(2, 4), oma = c(0, 0, 10, 0))
```

2. Build the histograms:

```
for(iCluster in 1:k2){
  tableClust <- dtClust[
    clusterHc2 == iCluster,
    table(output)
    ]
  sizeCluster <- dtClust[, sum(clusterHc2 == iCluster)]
  titlePie <- paste(sizeCluster, 'clients')
```

```
barplot(
  height = tableClust,
  names.arg = defPercentage(tableClust),
  col = c('blue', 'red'),
  main = titlePie
)
}
```

3. Add the title of the charts:

```
mtext(
  text = 'Hierarchic clustering, n = 7',
  outer = TRUE, line = 1, cex = 2
)
```

The histogram obtained is as follows:

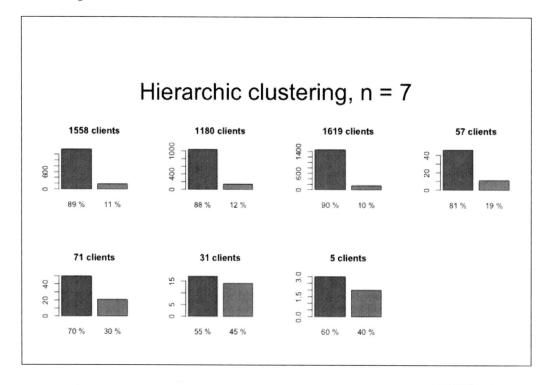

The first three clusters contain most of the clients and the marketing campaign hasn't been particularly effective on them. The fourth and fifth cluster has a significantly higher percentage of clients subscribing. The last two clusters are very successful although they are very small. The marketing campaign will start addressing all the new clients similar to the last two clusters and it will target a part of the clients of clusters four and five.

In conclusion, using clustering, we identified small groups of customers upon which the campaign has been very successful. However, most of the customers belong to a big cluster about which we don't have enough information. The reason is that the campaign is successful on a few customers with specific features.

# Predicting the output

The past marketing campaign targeted part of the customer base. Among other 1,000 clients, how do we identify the 100 that are keener to subscribe? We can build a model that learns from the data and estimates which clients are more similar to the ones that subscribed in the previous campaign. For each client, the model estimates a score that is higher if the client is more likely to subscribe. There are different machine learning models determining the scores and we use two well-performing techniques, as follows:

- **Logistic regression**: This is a variation of the linear regression to predict a binary output
- **Random forest**: This is an ensemble based on a decision tree that works well in presence of many features

In the end, we need to choose one out of the two techniques. There are cross-validation methods that allow us to estimate model accuracy (see *Chapter 6, Step 3 – Validating the Results*). Starting from that, we can measure the accuracy of both the options and pick the one performing better.

After choosing the most proper machine learning algorithm, we can optimize it using cross validation. However, in order to avoid overcomplicating the model building, we don't perform any feature selection or parameter optimization.

These are the steps to build and evaluate the models:

1. Load the `randomForest` package containing the random forest algorithm:

```
library('randomForest')
```

2. Define the formula defining the output and the variable names. The formula is in the format `output ~ feature1 + feature2 + ...`:

```
arrayFeatures <- names(dtBank)
arrayFeatures <- arrayFeatures[arrayFeatures != 'output']
formulaAll <- paste('output', '~')
formulaAll <- paste(formulaAll, arrayFeatures[1])
for(nameFeature in arrayFeatures[-1]){
  formulaAll <- paste(formulaAll, '+', nameFeature)
}
formulaAll <- formula(formulaAll)
```

3. Initialize the table containing all the testing sets:

```
dtTestBinded <- data.table()
```

4. Define the number of iterations:

```
nIter <- 10
```

5. Start a `for` loop:

```
for(iIter in 1:nIter)
{
```

6. Define the training and the test datasets:

```
indexTrain <- sample(
  x = c(TRUE, FALSE),
  size = nrow(dtBank),
  replace = T,
  prob = c(0.8, 0.2)
)
dtTrain <- dtBank[indexTrain]
dtTest <- dtBank[!indexTrain]
```

7. Select a subset from the test set in such a way that we have the same number of `output == 0` and `output == 1`. First, we split `dtTest` in two parts (`dtTest0` and `dtTest1`) on the basis of the output and we count the number of rows of each part (n0 and n1). Then, as `dtTest0` has more rows, we randomly select n1 rows. In the end, we redefine `dtTest` binding `dtTest0` and `dtTest1`, as follows:

```
dtTest1 <- dtTest[output == 1]
dtTest0 <- dtTest[output == 0]
n0 <- nrow(dtTest0)
n1 <- nrow(dtTest1)
dtTest0 <- dtTest0[sample(x = 1:n0, size = n1)]
dtTest <- rbind(dtTest0, dtTest1)
```

8. Build the random forest model using `randomForest`. The formula argument defines the relationship between variables and the data argument defines the training dataset. In order to avoid overcomplicating the model, all the other parameters are left as their defaults:

```
modelRf <- randomForest(
  formula = formulaAll,
  data = dtTrain
)
```

9.  Build the logistic regression model using `glm`, which is a function used to build **Generalized Linear Models (GLM)**. GLMs are a generalization of the linear regression and they allow to define a link function that connects the linear predictor with the outputs. The input is the same as the random forest, with the addition of `family = binomial(logit)` defining that the regression is logistic:

```
modelLr <- glm(
  formula = formulaAll,
  data = dtTest,
  family = binomial(logit)
)
```

10. Predict the output of the random forest. The function is `predict` and its main arguments are `object` defining the model and `newdata` defining the test set, as follows:

```
dtTest[, outputRf := predict(
  object = modelRf, newdata = dtTest, type='response'
)]
```

11. Predict the output of the logistic regression, using `predict` similar to the random forest. The other argument is `type='response'` and it is necessary in the case of the logistic regression:

```
dtTest[, outputLr := predict(
  object = modelLr, newdata = dtTest, type='response'
)]
```

12. Add the new test set to `dtTestBinded`:

```
dtTestBinded <- rbind(dtTestBinded, dtTest)
```

13. End the `for` loop:

```
}
```

We built `dtTestBinded` containing the `output` column that defines which clients subscribed and the scores estimated by the models. Comparing the scores with the real output, we can validate the model performances.

In order to explore `dtTestBinded`, we can build a chart showing how the scores of the non-subscribing clients are distributed. Then, we add the distribution of the subscribing clients to the chart and compare them. In this way, we can see the difference between the scores of the two groups. Since we use the same chart for the random forest and for the logistic regression, we define a function building the chart by following the given steps:

1. Define the function and its input that includes the data table and the name of the score column:

   ```
   plotDistributions <- function(dtTestBinded, colPred)
   {
   ```

2. Compute the distribution density for the clients that didn't subscribe. With `output == 0`, we extract the clients not subscribing, and using `density`, we define a `density` object. The adjust parameter defines the smoothing bandwidth that is a parameter of the way we build the curve starting from the data. The bandwidth can be interpreted as the level of detail:

   ```
   densityLr0 <- dtTestBinded[
     output == 0,
     density(get(colPred), adjust = 0.5)
     ]
   ```

3. Compute the distribution density for the clients that subscribed:

   ```
   densityLr1 <- dtTestBinded[
     output == 1,
     density(get(colPred), adjust = 0.5)
     ]
   ```

4. Define the colors in the chart using `rgb`. The colors are transparent red and transparent blue:

   ```
   col0 <- rgb(1, 0, 0, 0.3)
   col1 <- rgb(0, 0, 1, 0.3)
   ```

5. Build the plot with the density of the clients not subscribing. Here, `polygon` is a function that adds the area to the chart:

   ```
   plot(densityLr0, xlim = c(0, 1), main = 'density')
   polygon(densityLr0, col = col0, border = 'black')
   ```

6. Add the clients that subscribed to the chart:

   ```
   polygon(densityLr1, col = col1, border = 'black')
   ```

7.  Add the legend:

```
legend(
  'top',
  c('0', '1'),
  pch = 16,
  col = c(col0, col1)
)
```

8.  End the function:

```
  return()
}
```

Now, we can use `plotDistributions` on the random forest output:

```
par(mfrow = c(1, 1))
plotDistributions(dtTestBinded, 'outputRf')
```

The histogram obtained is as follows:

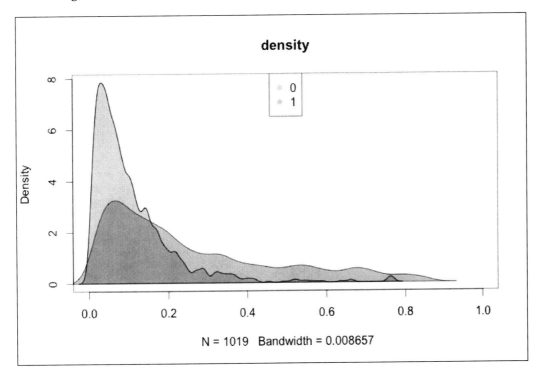

The x-axis represents the score and the y-axis represents the density that is proportional to the number of clients that subscribed for similar scores. Since we don't have a client for each possible score, assuming a level of detail of 0.01, the density curve is smoothed in the sense that the density of each score is the average between the data with a similar score.

The red and blue areas represent the non-subscribing and subscribing clients respectively. As can be easily noticed, the violet area comes from the overlapping of the two curves. For each score, we can identify which density is higher. If the highest curve is red, the client will be more likely to subscribe, and vice versa.

For the random forest, most of the non-subscribing client scores are between 0 and 0.2 and the density peak is around 0.05. The subscribing clients have a more spread score, although higher, and their peak is around 0.1. The two distributions overlap a lot, so it's not easy to identify which clients will subscribe starting from their scores. However, if the marketing campaign targets all customers with a score higher than 0.3, they will likely belong to the blue cluster. In conclusion, using random forest, we are able to identify a small set of customers that will subscribe very likely.

In order to get a comparison, we can build the same chart about the logistic regression output, as shown here:

```
plotDistributions(dtTestBinded, 'outputLr')
```

The histogram obtained is as follows:

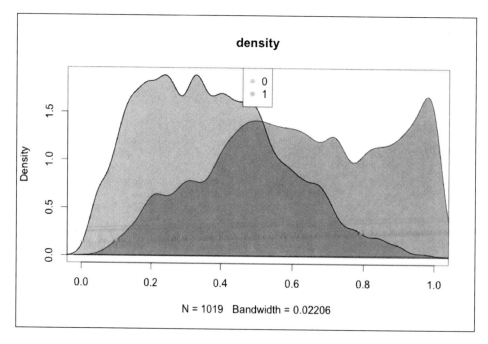

For the logistic regression, the two distributions overlap a bit, but they clearly cover two different regions and their peaks are very distant. The clients whose score is higher than 0.8 will very likely subscribe, so we can choose a small set of clients. We are also able to identify a bigger set of clients that will likely subscribe, if we choose the ones that scored above 0.5 or 0.6.

In conclusion, the logistic regression seems to have performed better. However, the distribution charts are good to just explore the performance and don't provide with a clear evaluation. The next step is to define how to evaluate the model using an index.

The validation index that we will use is the AUC and it depends on another chart that is the **Receiver Operating Characteristic (ROC)**. After building the classification model, we define a threshold and assume that the customers with a score above the threshold will subscribe. The ROC shows the model accuracy depending on the threshold. The curve dimensions are:

- **True positive rate**: This index shows out of the subscribing customers, which percentage has a score above the threshold. This index should be as high as possible.

- **False positive rate**: This index shows out of the non-subscribing customers, which percentage has a score above the threshold. This index should be as low as possible.

The **Area Under Curve (AUC)** is the area under the ROC. Given a random client that subscribed and another random client that did not subscribe, the AUC represents the probability that the score of the client that subscribed is higher than the other.

We can define a function that builds the chart and computes the AUC index:

1. Load the ROCR package containing the function used to cross validate the model:

   ```
   library('ROCR')
   ```

2. Define the function and its input that includes the data table and the name of the score column:

   ```
   plotPerformance <- function(dtTestBinded, colPred)
   {
   ```

3. Define a prediction object that is the starting point to build the ROC chart. The function is prediction and it is provided by the ROCR package:

   ```
   pred <- dtTestBinded[, prediction(get(colPred), output)]
   ```

4.  Build the ROC chart. The function provided by the ROCR package is `performance` and it allows you to evaluate the prediction in different ways. In this case, we want to build a chart with the `true` and `false` positive rates, so the input is **true positive rate (tpr)** and **false positive rate (fpr)**:

```
perfRates <- performance(pred, 'tpr', 'fpr')
plot(perfRates)
```

5.  Compute the AUC index using `performance`. The input is `auc` and it defines that we are computing the AUC index:

```
perfAuc <- performance(pred, 'auc')
auc <- perfAuc@y.values[[1]]
```

6.  Return the AUC index as the function output:

```
return(auc)
}
```

Using `plotPerformance`, we can build the chart about the random forest and we compute the `auc` index that we store in `aucRf`:

```
aucRf <- plotPerformance(dtTestBinded, 'outputRf')
```

The histogram obtained is as follows:

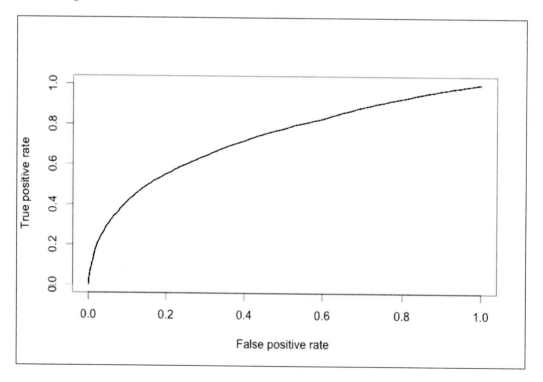

As anticipated, the chart displays the tpr and the fpr respectively. When the threshold is 1, no clients have a rate higher than it, so there are no positives (clients that are predicted to subscribe). In this situation, we are in the top-right corner and both the indices are equal to 100 percent. As the threshold decreases, we have more positive customers, so tpr and fpr decrease. In the end, when the threshold is 0, tpr and fpr are equal to 0 and we are in the bottom-left corner. In an ideal situation, tpr is equal to 1 and fpr is equal to 0 (top-left corner). Then, the closest the curve is to the top-left corner, the better.

Similar to the random forest, we build the chart and compute the AUC index for the logistic regression:

```
aucLr <- plotPerformance(dtTestBinded, 'outputLr')
```

The histogram obtained is as follows:

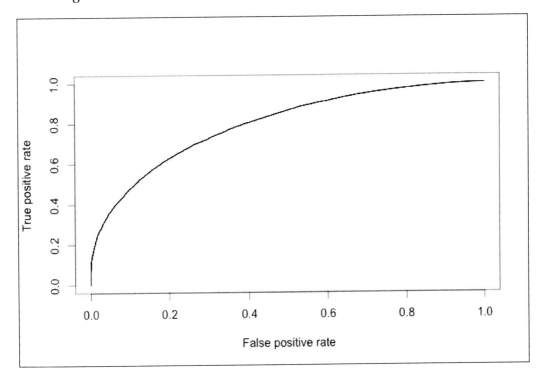

The chart for the logistic regression is similar to the one for the random forest. Looking at the details, we can notice that the curve in the bottom-left is steeper and at the top-right it is less steep, so the area under the curve, defining the AUC, is higher.

The cross validation contains a random component, so the AUC indices might vary a bit. Setting `nIter = 100`, the last time I executed the script the AUC was around 73 percent for the random forest and around the 79 percent for the logistic regression. We can conclude that the logistic regression performed better, so we should use it to build the model.

In this section, we learned how to build a model that provides a score for the customers. This algorithm allows the company to identify the customers that are more likely to subscribe and it is also possible to estimate its accuracy. A continuation of this chapter would be selecting a feature subset and optimizing the parameters in order to achieve better performances.

# Summary

In this chapter, you learned how to explore and transform the data related to a business problem. You used a clustering technique to segment the customer base of a bank and a supervised learning technique to identify a score ranking the clients. After building the machine learning model, you were able to cross validate it visualizing the ROC curve and computing the AUC index. In this way, you have been able to choose the most proper technique.

This book showed how machine learning models can solve business problems. Rather than just a tutorial, the book is a path showing the importance of machine learning, how to develop a solution, and how to solve a business problem using the techniques. I hope that the book has transmitted not only the machine learning concepts, but also the passion for a field that is at the same time valuable and fascinating. I'd like to thank you for following this path. I hope it is just the start of a wonderful journey.

Please don't hesitate to contact me if you have any queries.

# Index

## Thank you for buying
# R Machine Learning Essentials

## About Packt Publishing

Packt, pronounced 'packed', published its first book "*Mastering phpMyAdmin for Effective MySQL Management*" in April 2004 and subsequently continued to specialize in publishing highly focused books on specific technologies and solutions.

Our books and publications share the experiences of your fellow IT professionals in adapting and customizing today's systems, applications, and frameworks. Our solution based books give you the knowledge and power to customize the software and technologies you're using to get the job done. Packt books are more specific and less general than the IT books you have seen in the past. Our unique business model allows us to bring you more focused information, giving you more of what you need to know, and less of what you don't.

Packt is a modern, yet unique publishing company, which focuses on producing quality, cutting-edge books for communities of developers, administrators, and newbies alike. For more information, please visit our website: www.packtpub.com.

## About Packt Open Source

In 2010, Packt launched two new brands, Packt Open Source and Packt Enterprise, in order to continue its focus on specialization. This book is part of the Packt Open Source brand, home to books published on software built around Open Source licenses, and offering information to anybody from advanced developers to budding web designers. The Open Source brand also runs Packt's Open Source Royalty Scheme, by which Packt gives a royalty to each Open Source project about whose software a book is sold.

## Writing for Packt

We welcome all inquiries from people who are interested in authoring. Book proposals should be sent to author@packtpub.com. If your book idea is still at an early stage and you would like to discuss it first before writing a formal book proposal, contact us; one of our commissioning editors will get in touch with you.

We're not just looking for published authors; if you have strong technical skills but no writing experience, our experienced editors can help you develop a writing career, or simply get some additional reward for your expertise.

PUBLISHING    open source
community experience distilled

## Machine Learning with R

ISBN: 978-1-78216-214-8          Paperback: 396 pages

Learn how to use R to apply powerful machine learning methods and gain an insight into real-world applications

1.  Harness the power of R for statistical computing and data science.

2.  Use R to apply common machine learning algorithms with real-world applications.

3.  Prepare, examine, and visualize data for analysis.

## Learning Data Mining with R

ISBN: 978-1-78398-210-3          Paperback: 380 pages

Develop key skills and techniques within R to confidently create and customize data mining algorithms

1.  Develop a sound strategy for solving predictive modeling problems using the most popular data mining algorithms.

2.  Gain understanding of the major methods of predictive modeling.

3.  Packed with practical advice and tips to help you get to grips with data mining.

Please check **www.PacktPub.com** for information on our titles

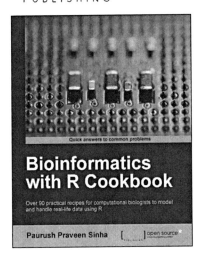

CPSIA information can be obtained
at www.ICGtesting.com
Printed in the USA
FSOW02n1236040315
5528FS

9 781783 987740